To the Lighthouse

Study Guide by Course Hero

What's Inside

👁 Book Basics 1

⊘ In Context 1

🖋 Author Biography 2

👫 Characters 3

📈 Plot Summary 7

🔍 Chapter Summaries 13

❝ Quotes 34

📣 Symbols 36

🔖 Themes 37

📖 Suggested Reading 38

👁 Book Basics

AUTHOR
Virginia Woolf

YEAR PUBLISHED
1927

GENRE
Drama

PERSPECTIVE AND NARRATOR
To the Lighthouse is told by a third-person omniscient narrator, with shifting points of view.

TENSE
To the Lighthouse is told in the past tense.

ABOUT THE TITLE
By going "to the" lighthouse—a symbol of the inaccessible—the characters strive to achieve what has previously been unattainable in *To the Lighthouse*.

⊘ In Context

Modernism

Queen Victoria's death and King Edward's accession to the throne in 1901 marked the beginning of the end of the Victorian era. Its ideals are reflected in the conventionality of Mr. and Mrs. Ramsay, whose marriage is scrutinized in *To the Lighthouse*. During the Edwardian era, from 1901 until King Edward's death in 1910, writers begin departing from the influences of 19th-century realism and naturalism, striving for a mode that represented a freer and more contemporary human spirit.

Woolf observed that human nature changed "on or about December 1910." By indicting past traditions and reinventing forms, artists looked at their subjects differently, often from multiple viewpoints. Stream of consciousness in literature reflected these modernist visions. Stream of consciousness, a term coined by psychologist William James, is a writing style where a character's thoughts and feelings are transmitted in a continuous uninterrupted flow. James Joyce, Virginia Woolf, and Marcel Proust were early pioneers of the form.

After the publication of *Mrs. Dalloway* in 1925, Woolf began writing *To the Lighthouse*, her fifth novel, which she published in 1927. As influential modernist and feminist works, the two novels remain her most popular and successful. Woolf insisted "books continue each other, in spite of our habit of judging them separately"; contemporary writer Hisham Matar, who counts *To the Lighthouse* as the novel in which Woolf "mastered" her sentence, sees this connection: "With each book she became more obsessed with language and how when we speak we often fall short of or else exceed what we intended to express." Woolf's sentences, "freely progressing, long, fractured series of observations and insights, unburdened and unhurried by the need to tell a 'story,'" examine the successes and failures of the human psyche and connection.

World War I

World War I (1914–18) left massive destruction and a devastating number of casualties. Woolf identified some events as indescribable: among these was war. In her diary she recorded the details and developments on the war front such as air raids, casualties, and sunken ships. Of the war, she said the "vast events now shaping across the channel are towering over us too closely and too tremendously to be worked [in] without a painful jolt in the perspective."

In England, with men away at war, women filled many positions at home. Woolf's sister-in-law, Ray Strachey, reported, "quiet mothers of families" and "flighty and giggling young girls" infiltrated the workforce, "transformed" into painters, ploughmen, engineers. Following the war, women had a foothold in life outside the home—rights and a voice—and were unwilling to retreat.

The second section of *To the Lighthouse,* "Time Passes" addresses the impact of the war, its massive destruction reflected in the deaths of family members and desolation of the Ramsays' lives and home. This section serves as a temporal bridge between past and present (prewar and postwar). Its conflated treatment of time, narrative distance, dramatic metaphor and understatement of death reflect Woolf's "indescribable."

Freud's Theories

Austrian neurologist Sigmund Freud (1856–1939) founded psychoanalysis, the treatment of mental illness through dialogue. Widely discussed during his lifetime, his theories, one of which was the idea of the Oedipus complex, interested Woolf, who explored his ideas of sexual development in *To the Lighthouse.* The complex is named after the Greek hero Oedipus, who in Sophocles's tragedy unknowingly marries his

mother and kills his father. The Oedipus complex explains a young child's sexual attraction to the parent of the opposite sex and the desire to remove the same-sex parent who blocks the child's fulfillment. The child's repression of sexual desire leads to the development of the superego, the part of the brain that acts as the conscience based on learned social standards.

According to Freud, not identifying with the same-sex parent may cause infantile neurosis. This trauma, which can be brought on by a parent's death or an unloving environment, may cause similar reactions to the same-sex parent in adulthood. At the novel's beginning, the Ramsays' son James feels murderous toward his father for demanding his mother's attention and for thwarting a trip to the lighthouse.

Mrs. Ramsay's death and its unresolved issues inflict trauma on her family and friends. The novel's structure suggests James's development is complicated. His love for his mother is frozen in time, and his conflict with his father continues. When his father finally compliments James's sailing as they reach the previously inaccessible lighthouse, his sister Cam thinks he has finally received what he has desired—his father's approval—suggesting resolution, growth, and development.

Author Biography

Adeline Virginia Stephen, later known as Virginia Woolf, was born into an artistic family on January 25, 1882, in London, England. Her father, Leslie Stephen was a well-known editor and biographer. Her mother, Julia Jackson Stephen, was a well-connected, good-natured woman, known for her beauty and modeling for pre-Raphaelite painters. Woolf began writing at an early age, spearheading a family newspaper, the *Hyde Park Gate News,* in which she heckled her older sister Vanessa, a painter, and her younger brother, Adrian, her mother's favorite as he was believed to be the most sensitive child.

Every summer the family vacationed on the Cornwall coast. In 1895, when Woolf was 13, her mother died at age 49. Shortly after Julia Stephen's death, Woolf suffered her first nervous breakdown. Deeply saddened and depressed, Woolf stopped writing for almost a year. As she began to emerge from her depression, her half sister, Stella Duckworth, died in 1897. When her father died in 1904, Woolf suffered another nervous breakdown.

During Woolf's recovery, Vanessa, Woolf's sister, moved the

Stephen children (Thoby, Virginia, Adrian, and herself) to the Bloomsbury section of London, where the siblings were free to pursue their intellectual and artistic interests.

During a family vacation in Greece in 1906, Woolf expressed her literary intentions, "I should like to write not only with the eye, but with the mind; & discover real things beneath the show." Shortly after this trip, Thoby died of typhoid fever, and Vanessa married art critic Clive Bell. Counting both events as losses, Woolf remained afloat, secretly writing *Reminiscences*, about her mother and her childhood.

Woolf wrote three novels, often called the St. Ives trilogy, inspired by her childhood summers in Cornwall: *Jacob's Room* (1922), *To the Lighthouse* (1927), and *The Waves* (1931). She represented those formative memories closely in *To the Lighthouse*, moving St. Ives Bay and the Godrevy Lighthouse to the Hebrides, and basing the novel on Julia and Leslie Stephen's marital dynamic in the characters of Mr. and Mrs. Ramsay, a traditional couple preserving the gender roles of a class-based society.

Both of Woolf's parents had children from previous marriages and spent summers with their eight children and friends at Talland House. Her father allowed Woolf access to his extensive library and because of him was surrounded by literary influences. Prominent writers such as Henry James, James Russell Lowell, and George Meredith frequented the Stephens' London and St. Ives homes.

Haunted by her mother's absence, Woolf wanted to write about her mother's life and death within the context of family summers. In "A Sketch of the Past" Woolf confessed her mother "obsessed" her: "I could hear her voice, see her, imagine what she would do or say as I went about my day's doings." The idea for *To the Lighthouse* came while she was strolling in Tavistock Square in Bloomsbury. She drafted the book in an "involuntary rush." After completing it Woolf declared she was no longer obsessed by her mother.

In 1905 Woolf and her family returned to Cornwall after an absence of 11 years, inspiring the third section of *To the Lighthouse*. Woolf found their "past preserved," as though "it had been guarded & treasured for us to come back to one day." On their arrival the caretaker cried at the memory of Julia Stephen's "beauty & charity," emphasizing the lasting effect Mrs. Stephen had on the community. That summer Woolf reflected on their train expedition, which was "more ... to fulfill a tradition than for the sake of any actual pleasure." Perhaps this

sensation is reflected in the novel through the thoughts of Cam and James Ramsay, who resent Mr. Ramsay's lighthouse expeditions, "rites he went through for his own pleasure in memory of dead people."

Between 1907 and 1930 the Bells and the Stephens hosted meetings of young artists and intellectuals. Inspired by the works of G.E. Moore, A.N. Whitehead, and Bertrand Russell, the Bloomsbury group, as it was known, discussed subjects related to art, literature, and philosophy. The group was interested in the meanings of goodness, truth, and beauty, and questioned conventional thinking. These meetings of the minds inspired Woolf to write both critically and creatively. Political theorist and writer Leonard Woolf, writer and critic Lytton Strachey, and novelist E.M. Forster were among their guests. Writers T.S. Eliot and Aldous Huxley also were associated with the group. In 1911 Leonard Woolf returned from eight years of government service in Ceylon (now Sri-Lanka), and he and Virginia married the following summer.

Plagued by loss and lack of confidence in her work, Virginia Woolf suffered bouts of depression throughout her life and attempted suicide multiple times. While working on *Between the Acts*, her final novel, despondent and unable to write, Virginia Woolf filled her pockets with stones and drowned herself in the River Ouse on March 28, 1941.

Characters

Mrs. Ramsay

The wife of Mr. Ramsay and mother of eight, Mrs. Ramsay is an advocate for marriage and family. She is deeply involved with her roles as wife, mother, hostess, benefactor, and muse. She supports the domestic and emotional needs of her husband, children, and guests and is particularly sensitive to her husband's continuing demands for reassurance and love. Mrs. Ramsay encourages women to fulfill society's traditional gender roles and believes marriage and family are necessary for fulfillment. Her unexpected death forces her family and friends to navigate the world without her, but she leaves a lasting influence on all.

Mr. Ramsay

Mrs. Ramsay's husband and father of eight, Mr. Ramsay published a significant book in his field at 25. After his early success, he has failed to gain more recognition. His lack of professional success has helped make him insufferably needy, irritable, and ill-tempered—traits he demonstrates by slamming doors, throwing plates, and other attention-grabbing, childish behavior. He constantly seeks praise and attention, especially from women: at 61 to ease the pain of his failures and at 71 to soothe the pain of heartbreak.

Lily Briscoe

Free-spirited Lily Briscoe is intense, thinking she is in love with the Ramsays, the island, the house, and perhaps Paul Rayley. Despite her independence and unwillingness to follow a traditional life, Lily is insecure about her work and her choices. She grows impatient with Charles Tansley, who insists women cannot be artists, and is envious of beautiful and seemingly serene Mrs. Ramsay, who appears to get everything she wants. Years later after Mrs. Ramsay's death, Lily returns to Scotland to confront her loss and paint her picture again, this time finishing it.

James

James Ramsay plays a key role in the novel because he is the character that wants to sail to the lighthouse as the novel begins. Always seeking to protect her children from disappointment, Mrs. Ramsay tries to preserve his sweet innocence by shielding him from his father's gruff, but accurate, comments about bad weather that will prevent the excursion. James carries a long and serious grudge toward his father, initially for stealing his mother's attention and later for not demonstrating love as his mother had.

Cam

Cam is rebellious, refusing to listen to her nursemaid and mother. Like Lily Briscoe, she is independent, but her youth prevents her independence from taking real form. Because of a later pact with James to withstand their father's dominance,

her neutrality causes conflict between the siblings as she relents in her resolve against their father, seeing him at his most charming. She shares in and understands James's pleasure when Mr. Ramsay finally compliments him for his sailing.

Paul Rayley

At Mrs. Ramsay's encouragement, simple and handsome Paul Rayley proposes to Minta Doyle, with whom he has been spending a lot of time. To Mrs. Ramsay's satisfaction, Paul is a refreshing alternative to academics, whom she finds boring. When Lily, who thinks she loves Paul, asks to accompany him to look for Minta's brooch, he laughs at her, hurting Lily's feelings.

Minta Doyle

A charismatic tomboy, Minta Doyle evokes Mrs. Ramsay's jealous feelings because of her youth, beauty, and Mr. Ramsay's attention. Fearless, Minta rushes into things with no thought of the consequences: wearing a precious heirloom to the beach, accepting Paul Rayley's proposal. These rash actions cause her pain (she cries over the brooch) and threaten the harmony of others (she is late to dinner and makes others late because they search for her brooch).

Character Map

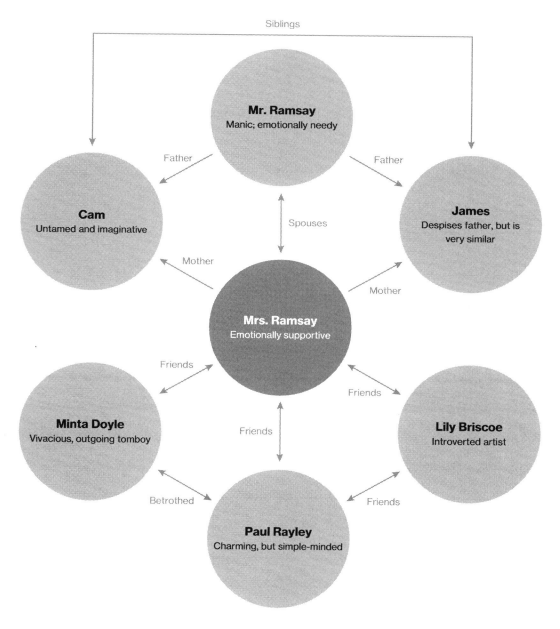

Full Character List

Character	Description
Mrs. Ramsay	Beautiful, kind, maternal, conventional Mrs. Ramsay is the novel's central character, with her influence extending to all others.
Mr. Ramsay	A metaphysical philosopher, insecure Mr. Ramsay can be unpleasant, harsh, and demanding.
Lily Briscoe	An independent and introverted artist, Lily Briscoe is Mrs. Ramsay's good friend and is painting a portrait of her and her youngest son, James.
James	The youngest of the Ramsays' eight children, James is fascinated by and wants to visit the lighthouse.
Cam	Free-spirited Cam Ramsay is the youngest of the Ramsays' daughters.
Paul Rayley	Serious, agreeable Paul Rayley is Minta Doyle's fiancé.
Minta Doyle	Outgoing, carefree, and charming, Minta Doyle stays with the Ramsays and becomes Paul Rayley's fiancée.
William Bankes	A childless widower, scrupulous William Bankes is a botanist, Mr. Ramsay's estranged friend, and Lily Briscoe's close friend; he is secretly in love with Mrs. Ramsay.
Mrs. Bast	Old Mrs. Bast helps Mrs. McNab clean the Ramsay house during its abandonment.
George Bast	George Bast is Mrs. Bast's son, who helps prepare the Ramsays' summer house after 10 years.
Mrs. Beckwith	Mrs. Beckwith, an elderly woman who sketches, is staying at the Ramsays' summer house in "The Lighthouse."
Aunt Camilla	Aunt Camilla is Mrs. Ramsay's beautiful aunt, who had a tendency to exaggerate.
Augustus Carmichael	Elderly, opium-smoking poet Augustus Carmichael, with his lack of grooming and inattention to others, is the only guest seemingly unaffected by Mrs. Ramsay; devastated by Andrew Ramsay's death, Carmichael writes war poetry that brings him fame.
Mrs. Carmichael	Although her name is not mentioned, Mrs. Carmichael is Augustus Carmichael's wife, who kicks him out and, in Mrs. Ramsay's opinion, turns her husband against her [Mrs. Ramsay].
Mrs. Doyle	Mrs. Doyle is Minta Doyle's mother, who hesitates to allow Minta to stay with the Ramsays, having heard Mrs. Ramsay is authoritarian and tyrannical.
Edward	Edward sends James a boar skull, which James nails to the wall.
Ellen	Ellen works for the Ramsays in the kitchen and brings Augustus Carmichael another plate of soup.
Elsie	Elsie is the impoverished woman Mrs. Ramsay visits in town.
Miss Giddings	Miss Giddings is a silly woman whom Mr. Ramsay once frightened when he shouted.
Uncle James	Mrs. Ramsay's Uncle James brought Mrs. Ramsay an opal necklace from India.
Kennedy	Kennedy is the Ramsays' former gardener, whom Mrs. Ramsay thought handsome but lazy; he was injured falling off a cart.
Macalister	Macalister accompanies Mr. Ramsay, James, and Cam on the excursion to the lighthouse.

Course Hero

Macalister's son	Macalister's quiet son fishes on the excursion to the lighthouse.
Davie Macdonald	Davie Macdonald is a former unreliable gardener for the Ramsays.
Carrie Manning	A friend of William Bankes, Carrie Manning is Mrs. Ramsay's estranged friend and Herbert Manning's wife, who has built a new billiard room.
George Manning	George Manning is a famous guest of the Ramsays, who liked Mrs. Ramsay.
Herbert Manning	Herbert Manning is Carrie Manning's successful husband and William Bankes's friend.
Marie	The Ramsays' Swiss maid, Marie cannot leave her job to be with her father, who is dying of cancer in Switzerland.
Marthe	Marthe works in the Ramsays' kitchen and serves the boeuf en daube at dinner.
Mrs. McNab	Mrs. McNab is the elderly caretaker for the Ramsays' summer house.
George McNab	George McNab is Mrs. McNab's son, who helps restore the Ramsays' summer house.
Nursemaid	The nursemaid tells Cam to give William Bankes a flower, and she refuses.
Mr. Paunceforte	A painter, Mr. Paunceforte visited and influenced landscape painting.
Andrew Ramsay	Gifted in mathematics, Andrew Ramsay is the Ramsays' oldest son; he is killed instantly during the war.
Jasper Ramsay	A bird hunter, Jasper is Mr. and Mrs. Ramsay's son.

Nancy Ramsay	Nancy Ramsay is the Ramsays' daughter, who accompanies Paul Rayley and Minta Doyle when he proposes and later forgets to order lunches for the lighthouse trip.
Prue Ramsay	The Ramsays' eldest and beautiful daughter, Prue, dies shortly after childbirth.
Roger Ramsay	Roger Ramsay is Mr. and Mrs. Ramsay's son.
Rose Ramsay	Rose Ramsay is Mr. and Mrs. Ramsay's daughter, who enjoys selecting jewelry for her mother to wear.
Sorley	Sorley is a father and the lighthouse keeper.
Sorley's son	Mrs. Ramsay knits stockings for Sorley's son, who has a tuberculous hip.
Charles Tansley	Narrow-minded, abrasive, sexist Charles Tansley admires Mr. Ramsay and comes to admire Mrs. Ramsay because of the attention she gives him and her embodiment of womanhood; his remarks that women cannot create art anger Lily.
Mr. Wallace	Mr. Wallace is a famous guest of the Ramsays, who liked Mrs. Ramsay.

Plot Summary

To the Lighthouse is divided into three parts, which are further broken down into numbered chapters. Virginia Woolf described the division as an H shape, the longer first and third "vertical" sections taking place during single days and the shorter "horizontal" connecting second part taking place over 10 years. These divisions illustrate the extension and contraction of time.

The Window

The story begins in early 1900s Scotland, just before World War I, as the Ramsays and company travel to their vacation home in the Hebrides. "The Window" covers about seven hours during an afternoon and evening but spans nearly half the novel. Mrs. Ramsay tells her six-year-old son, James, he can go to the lighthouse if the weather permits. Her husband, a metaphysician who made a significant contribution to the field early in his career, and his brash "admirer" Charles Tansley extinguish James's hopes by saying the weather will make it impossible. Later in the afternoon the Ramsays argue over the weather.

Family friend Lily Briscoe is attempting to paint a portrait of Mrs. Ramsay and James. William Bankes, another friend, living in the village, has agreed to stay for dinner. Mrs. Ramsay dedicates much of the day to protecting James's "fleeting" innocence and arranging a dinner party. Mr. Ramsay behaves boorishly, demanding female praise and reassurance. Throughout the day Mrs. Ramsay worries over the whereabouts of her daughter Nancy (who she thinks may be out walking with Minta Doyle, Paul Rayley, and Andrew Ramsay) and thinks about matchmaking and domestic issues like the greenhouse repair bill. Intermittently posing for Lily Briscoe's painting, Mrs. Ramsay devotes most of her time to ensuring the comfort of others, particularly her husband, within the house and in the community (the lighthouse keeper's ill son and poor Elsie in town).

The day culminates in the *bœuf en daube* supper for a group of 15 that includes newly engaged Minta Doyle and Paul Rayley. Mrs. Ramsay dedicates great effort to create a peaceful meal and thinks the event memorable, with Mr. Ramsay, despite his earlier ill temper, reciting a poem for her. This first part of the novel ends with Mr. and Mrs. Ramsay reading and talking quietly. She tells him he was right about the weather, her way of affirming her love.

Time Passes

The second part, "Time Passes," covers about 10 years in the span of a mere 10 to 20 pages or so. William Bankes, Lily Briscoe, Augustus Carmichael, and Andrew and Prue Ramsay arrive somberly at the summer house, as war begins across Europe. During one night Mrs. Ramsay dies unexpectedly. Prue

Ramsay marries and dies from childbirth complications. At war, Andrew Ramsay is killed instantly by a shell.

The house sits abandoned. Mrs. McNab cleans and tends to the house but during World War I closes it. After a decade the Ramsays write Mrs. McNab asking her to ready the house. She, along with Mrs. Bast, her son, and contractors, restore the summer home in time for the guests' arrival.

The Lighthouse

"The Lighthouse" covers only a few hours in one morning, focusing on the home's current state after a tumultuous decade. Lily Briscoe is unable to process all that has happened. Mr. Ramsay has planned a trip to the lighthouse and is angry his children have made them late for the trip. Lily recalls the painting of Mrs. Ramsay and James and decides to paint the scene again. When she sets up her easel outside, Mr. Ramsay interrupts her, seeking sympathy. Unable to comfort him, she remains silent until she notices his shoes. James and Cam Ramsay arrive, and the family leaves, while Lily feels remorse.

In the boat James and Cam are forced to confront their anger with Mr. Ramsay. On the lawn Lily is forced to confront her repressed emotions over the loss of her friend. After intense introspection, and Cam's change of heart, Cam and James reach the lighthouse together with their father; Lily finishes her painting.

Plot Diagram

Introduction

1. Mrs. Ramsay tells James he can visit the lighthouse.

Rising Action

2. Mr. Ramsay and Charles Tansley predict poor weather.

3. Lily Briscoe starts painting Mrs. Ramsay and James.

4. Mrs. Ramsay hosts a dinner party.

5. Mr. and Mrs. Ramsay realize Paul and Minta are engaged.

6. Mrs. Ramsay and her two eldest children die.

7. Mrs. McNab closes, then restores, the house.

8. Family and guests arrive at house after 10 years.

9. Lily Briscoe, highly emotional, works on a new painting.

10. Mr. Ramsay, Cam, and James leave for lighthouse.

Climax

11. Mr. Ramsay praises James.

Falling Action

12. The group arrives at the lighthouse.

13. Mr. Ramsay disembarks.

14. James and Cam follow Mr. Ramsay to the lighthouse.

Resolution

15. Lily Briscoe completes her painting.

Timeline of Events

Mid-September, about 1910

Mrs. Ramsay tells James he can visit the lighthouse the next day; Mr. Ramsay predicts bad weather.

Early evening

Lily Briscoe begins painting Mrs. Ramsay and James.

After 6 p.m.

William Bankes and Lily Briscoe stroll while Mr. Bankes vents about Mr. Ramsay.

Between 6 and 7 p.m.

Mr. Ramsay, embarrassed and angry, admits failure and seeks reassurance from his wife.

Shortly after

Lily Briscoe realizes William Bankes is in love with Mrs. Ramsay.

Dusk; before 7 p.m.

Paul Rayley proposes to Minta Doyle; Minta loses prized brooch.

Late evening

Dinner guests arrive; Mrs. Ramsay hosts.

Nearly midnight

Mr. Ramsay wants affection from Mrs. Ramsay, who tells him he was right about the weather.

At least a year later

Mrs. Ramsay dies unexpectedly during an autumn night.

Following spring

Prue Ramsay marries.

Summer, a year later

Prue Ramsay dies after childbirth; Andrew Ramsay dies at war.

Later during the war

Mrs. McNab closes the empty house she has been cleaning since Mrs. Ramsay's death.

September, about 1920

Mrs. McNab, with help, restores the house; Lily Briscoe and Mr. Carmichael arrive late at night.

Next morning about 8

Lily Briscoe remembers her painting.

Moments later

Lily Briscoe regrets failing to comfort Mr. Ramsay; he, Cam, and James leave for the lighthouse.

Same morning, still early

Lily Briscoe suffers an emotional episode.

Later that morning

Halfway to the lighthouse the boat stalls.

Lunchtime

Mr. Ramsay compliments James on his sailing; the group arrives at the lighthouse.

Moments later

Lily Briscoe completes her painting.

⌕ Chapter Summaries

Virginia Woolf wrote *To the Lighthouse* in three parts. This study guide provides a summary and analysis of each chapter within those parts.

The Window, Chapter 1

Summary

In the drawing room of her summer house on the Isle of Skye in the Hebrides, Mrs. Ramsay tells her son James, he can visit his beloved lighthouse in the morning if the weather permits. Looking out of the window, Mr. Ramsay says the weather will be poor. His wife reassures the disappointed James, saying she expects "it will be fine." To Mrs. Ramsay's frustration, Charles Tansley, her husband's disagreeable pupil, tests the wind with his hand and supports his mentor's opinion, disappointing James further. Mrs. Ramsay, always hospitable, then speaks with "severity" to her daughters as they mock Tansley for chasing them "all the way up to the Hebrides" when they would rather be alone. She tells Nancy, "He had been asked." Mrs. Ramsay's daughters dream of a "life different from hers; in Paris, perhaps," lives in which they are "not always taking care of some man or other."

Later Mrs. Ramsay asks Tansley, who admires her, to accompany her on an errand. On the way she asks Mr. Carmichael if he wants anything and then informs Tansley of Mr. Carmichael's "unfortunate marriage." He offers to carry her bag. She refuses. He wants her to see his successes, but a one-armed man posting an advertisement for a circus distracts her. When she asks Tansley if he has attended a circus, he talks about impoverished youth as she half-heartedly listens. She vows to stop making fun of him.

In town Mrs. Ramsay enjoys the sight of the bay, a favorite view of her husband's. While Mrs. Ramsay visits Elsie, Tansley waits in the foyer and vows to carry Mrs. Ramsay's bag. Taken with Mrs. Ramsay's beauty when she re-enters the room, he carries her things. As a worker admires her, Tansley experiences "pride," a new feeling for him.

Analysis

The novel begins *in media res*, in the middle of conflict, engaging readers immediately in a family problem: a disagreement over the weather. The stream-of-consciousness narrative, combined with interior monologue (the intimate thoughts, reactions, and emotions of characters), develops both conflict and characters. The shifting focus of the narrative point of view, moving from character to character, contributes to the novel's modernist aspects.

When Mr. Ramsay says the weather will not be favorable, James feels angry toward him for crushing his hope, and the conflict develops. James thinks, "Had there been an axe handy" or any weapon to kill his father with he "would have seized it," showing evidence of the rivalry for Mrs. Ramsay's love typified in Sigmund Freud's theory of the Oedipus complex. As Mrs. Ramsay restores James's hope, his love for his mother grows.

Mr. Ramsay's and Tansley's lack of consideration for James's feelings annoys Mrs. Ramsay, furthering the conflict. Tansley's character is complicated by his admiration for Mrs. Ramsay; he thinks she is the "most beautiful person he had ever seen." His affection for her motivates him to please her, and her attention comforts him, thus making his character more palatable to readers, if not to other characters. As Mrs. Ramsay spends time with him, her negative feelings wane and return, complicating their interactions.

In addition to the complex relationships in this section of the novel, its title, "The Window," draws attention to the characters' locations. Mrs. Ramsay and James sit in the drawing room while Mr. Ramsay and Tansley engage with them through the window during their walk and discussion. This placement creates an opposition, which might represent gender roles. Mrs. Ramsay, mother and wife, remains in the house. Her husband and his male student find their place outside, near the home but not constricted by it. Where women have the house, men have the rest of the world. This difference creates tension that looms around the roles of Mrs. Ramsay and other female characters.

Finally, "The Window," the longest of the three parts of the novel, addresses events that cover about seven hours of time. Stylistically, Woolf anchors time through events and experiences in the characters lives rather than anchoring time to the traditional calendar or clock. She stretches or compresses time through the length of the narrative to suggest the significance and effects of particular events on the lives of the characters. While *To the Lighthouse* takes place over 10 years, it also takes place over the course of one day or one 24-hour period. "The Window" covers an afternoon and an evening; "Time Passes" covers a dark night that spans 10 years; and "The Lighthouse" covers a morning.

The Window, Chapter 2

Summary

From the window, an unidentified man tells James with "some semblance of geniality" there will be no trips to the lighthouse the next day. Mrs. Ramsay is annoyed he continues to disappoint James. She thinks of him as an "odious little man" and wonders, "Why go on saying that?"

Analysis

Because Mrs. Ramsay calls the unidentified man "odious," readers assume it is Tansley as she calls his harping on and upsetting her youngest child "odious" in the previous chapter. Although his changed nature—attempted "geniality"—displays his growing feelings for Mrs. Ramsay, his nature also damages the progress they made on their walk, developing the awkwardness of his character as well as Mrs. Ramsay's inaccessibility.

The Window, Chapter 3

Summary

Mrs. Ramsay slicks James's hair and whispers about the possibilities of sunshine. Searching a catalog for lawn equipment, she listens to the sounds of the children playing outside, Mr. Ramsay and Tansley's chatter, and the waves. Usually the sound of the sea calms her, but sometimes her mind wanders to the "destruction of the island and its engulfment in the sea."

When she hears a foreign sound—a "thundered hollow"—she

grows tense. Assuming she heard it only because Tansley had left, she feels comforted by the sounds of Mr. Ramsay walking the terrace. A moment later she hears a "loud cry" and checks whether anyone else has heard. She discovers Lily Briscoe, who also heard the sound, painting at the lawn's edge and remembers to pose for the portrait Lily is painting of her.

Analysis

Mrs. Ramsay's protection of James's budding "passion" for the lighthouse shows her maternal nature and level of involvement in daily tasks. This minute attention develops the theme of love and loss and foreshadows the void her absence will leave. Restoring James's hope of boating to the lighthouse, which comes to symbolize inaccessibility, shows her hope of preserving her youngest child's innocence.

As Mrs. Ramsay sorts through background noise, her impression of what she hears and the ensuing emotions emphasize her character. Her fixation on the waves, which now bring thoughts of catastrophe, reflects her troubled state of mind, how close she is to negative emotions. Her continual edginess creates tension. Mrs. Ramsay forgets about posing for Lily, showing her preoccupation with domestic responsibilities and her own thoughts. However, even though she does not take Lily's painting "very seriously," she still sits for the portrait, showing how much she desires to please others.

The Window, Chapter 4

Summary

As Lily Briscoe paints outdoors on the lawn, she fears someone might look at her work. Mr. Ramsay, running around outdoors, enacting and reciting poetry, almost knocks down her easel and says, "Some one had blundered," glaring at her and William Bankes standing nearby. Mr. Bankes suggests he and Lily take a walk. Lily agrees. As she stores her brushes, she contemplates craft and her frustration with her inability to recreate what she envisions.

Their "usual" route takes them to a view of the bay, where they find excitement in watching the waves. When Bankes gazes at the distant sand dunes, he thinks of Mr. Ramsay and is sad they grew apart after Mr. Ramsay married.

Returning to the house, Mr. Bankes speaks of his envy of the Ramsays, and Lily asks him to consider Mr. Ramsay's work. He appreciates her advice and admits he thinks of Mr. Ramsay's success often. Although the metaphysician's career peaked before 40, Mr. Bankes admits making a contribution is rare. Overwhelmed by her feelings for Mr. Bankes—thinking he is the "finest human being" she knows—Lily is, simultaneously, discouraged by his flaws, someone who "knows nothing about trifles." Mr. Ramsay shouts again, "Some one had blundered," then slams the door in their faces.

Analysis

Lily Briscoe interacts with Mr. Ramsay and Mr. Bankes with different results. She is relieved when Mr. Ramsay, whom she considers "ridiculous" and "alarming," ignores her painting. Yet, as William Bankes approaches, she is glad to see him, feeling no impulse to hide her work. That William Bankes is the only person who would not cause her to "turn her canvas upon the grass" shows their level of comfort with one another. Her struggle with painting, recreating her vision, develops the theme of reality versus the ideal, as she cannot achieve the essence she has in mind.

Through the closeness and interactions between Lily Briscoe and William Bankes, Woolf explores the theme of love and loss. On their walk, Mr. Bankes talks through his lost platonic love, Mr. Ramsay. As childless widower, Mr. Bankes also represents lost romantic love. Lily, an artist, admits to being "in love with them all, in love with this world." Lily suffers knowing the limitations of a class-based and gender-based society. She is aware of how others see her ("her own inadequacy, her insignificance, keeping house for her father off the Brompton Road"); her past and present draw attention to her future—will she marry? will she paint?—as she opposes Charles Tansley, who believes women cannot create art, and Mrs. Ramsay, who thinks marriage and children are a woman's highest honor. As Mr. Bankes confides in Lily, she gushes over his "goodness," but believes "praise would be an insult" to him. Thus, displaying quiet longing. Lily fails to connect with even her closest, nonjudgmental friend as he confides in her.

The Window, Chapter 5

Summary

As Lily Briscoe and William Bankes walk by, Mrs. Ramsay tells James if the weather keeps them from the lighthouse, they can go another day. Mrs. Ramsay is suddenly struck with the idea of Lily and William marrying. She measures the stocking she is knitting against James, who fidgets.

Observing her surroundings, she notices how "shabby" everything looks. Quickly, she shakes the thought away because her family loves the house. Overwhelmed by the books she has no time to read, she considers solutions to improve the house's appearance. Open windows remind her of Marie, their maid, whose father is dying.

Mrs. Ramsay scolds James for moving. When she discovers the stocking is short, she is sad. As Mrs. Ramsay returns to knitting, and Mr. Bankes admires her beauty, she kisses James and tells him he can cut out more pictures.

Analysis

Mrs. Ramsay's sudden "admirable idea" of Lily and Mr. Bankes marrying indicates her support of marriage, as a social convention, rather than an understanding of people. Despite her upholding the social structure, the immediate action of getting James to stop fidgeting (wondering "what demon possessed him") and the growing list of tasks create tension. After realizing she must knit more, the narrator repeats, "Never did anybody look so sad," highlighting her exhaustion, as Mr. Bankes ponders her beauty and her seeming unawareness of it. He thinks, "she's no more aware of her beauty than a child." He thinks perhaps "her beauty" bores her, remembering how she wears deerstalker hats outside to fetch children. A practical and busy woman, Mrs. Ramsay does not cultivate her beauty; in fact, it seems of little interest to her, whereas it awes others.

In this chapter, Marie serves to develop the theme of reality versus the ideal. Her father suffers from throat cancer in Switzerland while she works as a maid on a Scottish island. Her fixation with the ideal, the distant Swiss mountains, illustrates her wish to be home with her dying father, whereas reality keeps her where she is. Marie's reality is class related; she needs to work, and her position prevents her from spending time with her dying father. The situation reflects the theme of love and loss, as well. Marie is losing her father, whom she loves.

Also, Mrs. Ramsay thinks, he's "leaving them fatherless." This somber realization foreshadows Mrs. Ramsay's sudden death and furthers the theme of love and loss, illustrating the children, Marie and the eight Ramsay children, who will lose a parent.

The Window, Chapter 6

Summary

In the drawing room Mr. Ramsay repeats, "Some one had blundered," angrily recalling his encounter with William Bankes and Lily Briscoe. His wife sees he is "outraged and anguished" as she smooths James's hair. Mr. Ramsay tickles James, who rebuffs him.

Mr. and Mrs. Ramsay argue about the weather. Mrs. Ramsay insists there is "nothing" to say. When he volunteers to visit the Coastguard for more information, her mood toward him changes suddenly—"She was not good enough to tie his shoe strings, she felt"—and Mr. Ramsay calms down. After he pesters James a last time, Mr. Ramsay returns to the terrace.

From outside he glimpses his wife and son and returns to his thoughts. Using the alphabet as an analogy for intellectual achievement, he ponders his next feat, R. Dividing thinkers into two classes—those who conquer the alphabet one letter at a time and those who see the entire alphabet at once—he admits he is not a "genius" (understanding it at once) and ponders the rarity of someone achieving Z. Thinking of fame and failure, he stops at the window to gaze again at his wife and son, who return his gaze.

Analysis

Mrs. Ramsay's failure to understand Mr. Ramsay's "poetic" melodrama shows their differences. She focuses on his face, trying to understand him, but finds his repetitive phrases "ridiculous" and pays more attention to James, displaying her

priorities. James's animosity toward his father continues, which shows a universal stage of development in the Freud's oedipal theory. Six-year-old James highlights his father's difficult character. The demands of both her husband and son wear on Mrs. Ramsay; she describes herself as a "sponge sopped full of human emotions."

During moments of anger, Mr. Ramsay directs his hostility toward his wife's optimism at all women, thinking the "folly of women's minds enraged him." Although Mrs. Ramsay is assertive, defending herself and telling him to stop, she feels unworthy of him, demonstrating how traditional attitudes of women's subservience to men govern her thoughts and feelings.

Yet their relationship is not without tender moments. Mr. Ramsay glances at Mrs. Ramsay while he thinks outside: she is his touchstone. His character is complicated as he comes to terms with his professional failure. Mr. Ramsay's insight gives credence to Mr. Bankes's observations. Mr. Ramsay's bulging forehead vein shows how much he wants another success, further developing the internal conflicts of his character.

The Window, Chapter 7

Summary

James Ramsay hates his father for interrupting his mother, who reads to him while she knits. He hopes his father will leave, but Mr. Ramsay lingers, "demanding sympathy." He tells his wife he is a "failure," looking at her expectedly. Her mention of Charles Tansley's admiration fails to soothe him. James senses his mother gathering strength as she tells his father to relax. Mr. Ramsay repeats himself, and Mrs. Ramsay, "spent," comforts her "egotistical" husband.

Rejuvenated, he volunteers to watch their children play cricket. She returns to the story. Physically and mentally exhausted, Mrs. Ramsay thinks about the "origin" of her mental state. Disturbed by the lie he cornered her into telling him, she acknowledges the truth; she is worried about money, his recent failures, and the "burden" of shielding the children from everything. Augustus Carmichael arrives.

Analysis

Mrs. Ramsay naively tries to hide things from her children, while James perceives the energy his father's demands cost her. The situation creates conflict and dramatic irony, as readers are aware of James's knowledge, but Mrs. Ramsay is not. James's hatred reflects Freud's Oedipal theories; the young boy resents his father for stealing his mother's attention, which he wants for himself. However, Mr. Ramsay is in some ways as infantile and dependent as a child, and readers may observe he wants his wife's attention in a childish, rather than an adult, way.

James's concern about his mother's body, from "sitting loosely" to becoming a "rosy-flowered fruit tree laid with leaves and dancing boughs," is Oedipal, intensified with the voicing of the death wish: James describes his father as a sword that stabs and kills his mother.

The symbolic tree (in this case, Mrs. Ramsay) represents love, life, and connection. After the manipulative encounter in which she must support her husband's ego, she is described, again, flower-like—shutting. The multiple images develop conflict in Mrs. Ramsay's character as one that provides love, life, and connection and at the same time feels there is "scarcely a shell of herself left for her to know herself by."

The Window, Chapter 8

Summary

Augustus Carmichael avoids Mrs. Ramsay, behavior Mrs. Ramsay thinks results from his wife's dislike of her. Mrs. Ramsay considers her encounters with other "famous" men. Aware of her beauty and effect on people, Mrs. Ramsay is offended by Mr. Carmichael's attitude, but she acknowledges her "vanity." Augustus Carmichael retreats to a "corner," causing "snubbed" Mrs. Ramsay to ponder the "pettiness" of human interactions—how social situations are "flawed," "despicable," and "self-seeking at ... best"—while reading to James.

Mr. Ramsay fails to watch the children outside. Instead, he reads about the popularity of Shakespeare's home, trying to demean the arts by creating an argument against expression.

He watches at the bay, smoking and meditating on ignorance and the lectures he will present to students in Cardiff. Gazing at his wife and son in the window, he admits his falseness in "talking nonsense," and the fragility of his ego.

Lily Briscoe packs up her art supplies, thinking Mrs. Ramsay accommodates her husband too readily. As she watches Mr. Ramsay, she imagines the shock he must feel transitioning from his thoughts as they talk "nonsense" and play games.

Analysis

Mr. Carmichael's presence makes Mrs. Ramsay consider the shallowness of socialization, as her role is caretaker for all who stay at the house. Mrs. Ramsay goes "out of her way" to please people, especially guests. Yet these interactions are not completely altruistic because she likes feeling needed. She admits she likes to "help" and "give," so people might praise, "need," "admire," and call on her, saying "O Mrs. Ramsay! dear Mrs. Ramsay ... Mrs. Ramsay, of course!" The attention she pays to James, a "bundle of sensitiveness," illustrates this "vanity" because James, in this Oedipal stage, prefers her to anyone, especially his father.

In exploring his thoughts on the arts and his upcoming lecture, Mr. Ramsay admits the argument he intends to develop is self-serving and supports an intellectual hierarchy that enforces his power in a male-dominated intellectual world.

The chapter focuses on the idea of nonsense, which arises from lack of success. Characters feel the lack of success and suffer emotionally in different ways: Mrs. Ramsay cannot connect with Mr. Carmichael, Lily struggles with her painting, and Mr. Ramsay's career has stalled. The gap between what the characters have achieved and what they would like to have achieved develops the theme of reality versus the ideal.

The Window, Chapter 9

Summary

As Mr. Ramsay stomps off, William Bankes consoles Lily Briscoe, unnerved by Mr. Ramsay's mood swing. Mr. Bankes agrees that Mr. Ramsay's unconventional behavior is upsetting. When Mr. Bankes suggests Mr. Ramsay behaves hypocritically,

Lily disagrees, saying his neediness is genuine. Lily says she is disturbed not by his behavior, but his "narrowness." While Lily ventures into thought—admiring the "penetrating and exciting" love between Mr. and Mrs. Ramsay—Mr. Bankes wishes she would agree with him.

While watching Mr. Ramsay walk to the bay, Lily considers his strengths and weaknesses. She ponders how life's "little separate incidents ... became curled and whole like a wave." Knowing Mr. Bankes awaits, she begins to criticize Mrs. Ramsay but stops when she sees Mr. Bankes look with rapture at Mrs. Ramsay inside the window. She is moved by his emotion and Mrs. Ramsay's power. She thinks about what she wanted to say about Mrs. Ramsay, who believes "an unmarried woman has missed the best of life." Thinking Mrs. Ramsay is mistaken, Lily sees herself as not made for marriage and seeks fulfillment and connection with others through her art.

Mr. Bankes then turns his attention to Lily's painting, making her self-conscious, for she thinks her painting is not very good. He questions her artistic intentions, and the discussion leads to her opinions on light and shadows. The discussion interests Mr. Bankes, a scientist. With his attention, Lily decides not to elaborate, removes her canvas from the easel, and happily contemplates the "profoundly intimate" revelation regarding Mr. Bankes's love for Mrs. Ramsay.

Analysis

Lily Briscoe's thoughts display her rich internal life, a theme of the novel. She often refers to her insignificance, not wanting to "bore" Mr. Bankes, yet her vibrant musings and keen observations about herself and others make her, arguably, the novel's most insightful, honest, and open character.

Here in Lily's mind, readers observe an earlier interaction between Mrs. Ramsay and Lily. Mrs. Ramsay, who supports marriage and procreation, pushes Minta Doyle as well as Lily to marry. Lily's refusal to marry creates tension: why should she, as she has a father, a home, and her painting. She prefers being "alone" and doesn't want a house "full of children." While Mrs. Ramsay thinks Lily is a "fool," Lily laughs long and "hysterically" at her friend, who calmly governs over "destinies" she doesn't "understand," developing both female characters.

While Mrs. Ramsay represents Victorian ideals with her "simple certainty," Lily, who knows "she was not made for that,"

represents modern women. Yet Lily still thinks highly of her friend, who she suspects thinks she is a "much younger" and "insignificant" person. Charles Tansley's sexist opinion about women creators and Mrs. Ramsay's conventional beliefs instill Lily with doubts. Lily's interior life explores her defense for living the life she wants. These doubts infiltrate her painting, which she finds "infinitely bad."

The Window, Chapter 10

Summary

As Cam Ramsay runs past Lily Briscoe and William Bankes, Mrs. Ramsay calls her to deliver a message to the cook. Mrs. Ramsay wants to know whether Andrew, Minta Doyle, and Paul Rayley have returned from their postlunch walk. When Cam says they have not, Mrs. Ramsay, who thinks Paul and Minta should marry, believes the good-natured but not brilliant Paul has proposed.

In the house, Mrs. Ramsay continues reading to James. Because Minta is staying with her, Mrs. Ramsay, conventional in her views on proper social behavior, considers herself responsible to Minta's parents, who were reluctant to let their unconventional daughter stay with the Ramsays because an unnamed woman had once accused Mrs. Ramsay of stealing her daughter's "affections." Mrs. Ramsay worries about her own outward appearances and gossip and is concerned about Minta's walks with Paul Rayley. In thinking of the hurtful accusation, Mrs. Ramsay reflects on her choices and behavior in influencing people, her halted dreams, and her wishes that her children stay young and happy—"for ever just as they were, demons of wickedness, angels of delight." "Feeling life rather sinister again," Mrs. Ramsay experiences guilt over influencing Minta's choice. She wonders if she is "wrong" in suggesting Minta, "only twenty-four," marry, knowing "too quickly" she had, "almost as if it [marrying and having children] were an escape for her too."

As the light wanes, Mrs. Ramsay thinks again about Paul, Minta, and Andrew, who have not yet returned. When she finishes reading to James, she looks at the lighthouse—now lit. Before James has a chance to ask about visiting it again, Mildred takes him away.

Analysis

Lily Briscoe's easel is grazed again, this time by Cam, the "wild" one. This repetitive action could signify how Lily's art is devalued because she is a woman. (No one interrupts the men talking on the terrace.) Initially Cam ignores her mother, who wonders what she is thinking about. Cam's disobedience reflects the distance between her and her mother, whereas James and Mrs. Ramsay seem inseparable, reflecting the dynamics of the parent/child relationships as seen in a Freudian context. In the house Mrs. Ramsay shoos Cam, displaying preference for James's company. After Cam leaves, Mrs. Ramsay is "relieved," for she and James share the same tastes and are comfortable together. Cam's rebellious nature likens Cam to Lily, who doesn't value Mrs. Ramsay's ideals for herself (marriage and children). Mrs. Ramsay's thoughts about Minta and Paul illustrate social expectations for women. Because of how much time Minta and Paul spend alone, Paul is considered a suitor, and Minta is expected to marry him. In Mrs. Ramsay's mind, Minta's excessive time alone with Paul could damage her reputation.

Mrs. Ramsay's warm feelings toward Paul display her aversion to the "clever men" of her husband's circle, building tension and revealing details about the Ramsays. To Mr. Ramsay, his wife's "pessimistic" views are a source of contention. While Mrs. Ramsay tends to believe life is "sinister," Mr. Ramsay is "more hopeful" and "happy," possibly because of the attention and admiration he forces all to give him.

The Window, Chapter 11

Summary

Mrs. Ramsay looks at the pictures James has cut from the catalog, thinking "children never forget," as she reflects that James will always remember his disappointment at his father's words confirming the trip to the lighthouse will not take place. The situation causes her to say to herself, "We are in the hands of the Lord," a statement she regrets, thinking she was forced to say it. She is relieved to be alone, having only to think of herself. Knitting, she thinks of foreign places and of the unhappiness of the world. Periodically watching the lighthouse's beam, Mrs. Ramsay grows annoyed with her thoughts and continues to knit, contemplating the world's pain.

As her husband observes her, he feels saddened by her remoteness, his inability to "protect" her, and his constant demands on her that worsen her mental state. Knowing "sound" or "sight" fights solitude, Mrs. Ramsay searches for a sound but hears only the sea. Observing her again, Mr. Ramsay wants to talk to her but leaves her alone. Mrs. Ramsay, knowing he wants to "protect" her, follows him, taking her shawl.

Analysis

James's cuttings, including a refrigerator, lawn mower, and man in a suit, hint at a conflict, developing tension about the Ramsays' financial and household concerns. Throughout "The Window" Mrs. Ramsay worries about the 50-pound greenhouse repair; these items may allude to the emotional and/or financial tensions surrounding the acquisition of more modern appliances and the expense of maintaining a vacation home on top of feeding, clothing, and educating eight children. While the interior life of most characters may be more comforting than external daily life, Mrs. Ramsay's interior life is not. Her personal thoughts are dark, whereas her outer life is light. The solitude of her interior life contradicts her exterior life in which she is surrounded by admirers and involved in their lives. In fact, others see her presence connected with light, but twice she describes herself as a "wedge of darkness," evoking the image of her in Lily Briscoe's painting, which represents Lily's understanding of her.

Unable to recall the origin of her thoughts, Mrs. Ramsay feels "trapped into saying something she did not mean." The repetition and falseness of "We are in the hands of the Lord"—she thinks, "How could any Lord have made this world?—illustrates her mental state. As the narrative switches between husband and wife, the couple appears united. She correctly intuits Mr. Ramsay's desire to protect her, thus her following him instead of being alone as she wishes to be; Mr. Ramsay knows his neediness wears his wife down.

The Window, Chapter 12

Summary

Outside Mrs. Ramsay talks about how handsome their gardener Kennedy is. Seeing the ladder against the greenhouse, she decides against bringing up the repair cost. Mrs. Ramsay is concerned about Jasper Ramsay shooting birds, but her husband insists he will grow out of it. The two discuss Charles Tansley and his objectionable attributes and hope he does not pursue Prue. Mr. Ramsay, whom Tansley worships, says he (Tansley) is "not a polished specimen." They disagree on Andrew Ramsay. Mr. Ramsay wishes Andrew would apply himself, but Mrs. Ramsay is happy whether he does or does not. Mr. Ramsay tells his wife not to worry about Minta Doyle and Paul Rayley, still not back from their walk. When she asks him what he wanted to tell her—hoping for an apology following their earlier disagreement—he confesses he hates seeing her "sad." Uncomfortable about her husband witnessing this emotion, the dutiful wife avoids eye contact. He wants to return to his thoughts, alone.

Missing long walks in the sand dunes, he says if the weather permits he might go for a walk. Although doubting him, she acknowledges his wish. He looks at the sea, the erosion, and moans, "Poor little place," annoying Mrs. Ramsay.

He kisses her hand. She sees a star and wants to show him but stops because he is not an observer of such things. He pretends to look at the flowers, and she knows he is pretending. When Mrs. Ramsay sees William Bankes and Lily Briscoe walking, she thinks they should marry.

Analysis

Mr. and Mrs. Ramsay's conversation builds tension as their differences and disagreements become more apparent. Mr. Ramsay accuses Mrs. Ramsay of their daughters' embellishing stories, saying they learn it from her. They disagree over scholarships for Andrew. Yet the couple develops the theme of love and loss by showing one another little graces. For example, on the verge of saying Charles Tansley is the only person who likes his book, Mr. Ramsay stops himself. Mrs. Ramsay decides against telling Mr. Ramsay the cost of the greenhouse repairs. Even though they are annoyed with their differences, their disagreements do "not matter." For the most part, they seem to appreciate their differences; she enjoys his enthusiasm about scholarships, and he likes her to be "proud

of Andrew whatever he did."

In response to Mr. Ramsay's "phrase-making," Mrs. Ramsay thinks about suicide. Supposing she said "half" the things her husband said, she thinks "she would have blown her brains out by now." This statement alludes to mental health issues, deepening the conflict because Mr. Ramsay is concerned and Mrs. Ramsay is self-conscious about her sadness. The reference foreshadows her death.

The Window, Chapter 13

Summary

While walking on the lawn, William Bankes and Lily Briscoe discuss travel and art—he has visited Amsterdam, Madrid, and Rome; she, Brussels, Paris, and Dresden. Lily thinks "perhaps it was better not to see pictures." They see the Ramsays looking at the children playing ball. Reflecting on an earlier conversation with Mrs. Ramsay, who wants Lily to marry, Lily understands marriage as a "man and a woman looking at a girl throwing a ball."

Mrs. Ramsay smiles at them, happy she has convinced Mr. Bankes to stay for dinner. While watching Prue catch the ball, Mrs. Ramsay asks after the walking party and then after Nancy.

Analysis

William Bankes attempts to connect with Lily Briscoe by discussing the art he has encountered. Instead she ponders the lack of art she has seen. She considers this lack a positive because viewing famous pictures makes her "hopelessly discontented," preventing her from painting, which for her has great importance. The discussion highlights their lack of real connection—the observer and the creator.

When Mr. Bankes supposes, "We can't all be Titians and we can't all be Darwins," Lily wishes she could compliment him, but thinks he—unlike most men—is not seeking one. After much silence, Lily insists, regardless of success, she will always paint. These thoughts develop the theme of internal life as it is more vivid than the conversation. In addition, they highlight Lily's perceived need to please, as a woman aware of her role despite her rejection of it.

The Window, Chapter 14

Summary

Nancy Ramsay reluctantly accompanies Minta Doyle on the walk only because she asks her expectedly with "her dumb look." Nancy does not want to be "drawn into it all." On their way Andrew observes Minta; he approves of her sensible clothing and rashness but worries her fearlessness (she is afraid only of bulls) might lead her "to kill herself in some idiotic way." Andrew dislikes Paul Rayley's habit of calling him "old fellow" and "clapping him on the back."

At the beach Andrew goes to the Pope's Nose. Nancy searches for sea anemones in the pools. Paul and Minta—alone—stay on the beach. Nancy broods, rendered motionless by the "intensity" of her "feelings" of "nothingness." When the tide rises, Andrew yells the sea is rising. Andrew and Nancy walk away from the shore, witnessing Paul and Minta in an embrace.

On the cliff top Minta realizes she has lost her grandmother's heirloom brooch. They return to search for it but without luck, Andrew feeling annoyed at having to do this and even more annoyed with Minta's outburst about her fear of the tide and loss of the brooch. During their return Paul comforts Minta, who weeps, and promises to go back at dawn despite the danger. Paul vows to find the brooch or buy her another. Contemplating his and Minta's future together, Paul plans to speak with Mrs. Ramsay, who "made him" propose, made him feel as though he could do anything. As they arrive back at the house, he notices the lights are on. They are late.

Analysis

Because of the shifting points of view and stream of consciousness, much of the novel's action and conflict are internal. External action is often noted within parentheses or brackets, setting it aside from characters' internal lives. The entire chapter is enclosed in parentheses. Mrs. Ramsay has been worrying about the group and isn't sure where Nancy is; this chapter provides an external explanation.

It seems Nancy and Andrew are invited on Minta and Paul's walks as easygoing, or inattentive, chaperones. Andrew's and Nancy's annoyance with Minta and Paul develops tension. The Ramsay children, uninterested in Minta and Paul's romantic relationship and in each other, go off by themselves individually, but they share in commiseration, thinking they "had not wanted this horrible nuisance to happen." They dislike Minta and Paul all the more.

On the trip there Minta holds and releases Nancy's hand often, and Nancy watches the town from the cliff. Both actions create more distance between them. Andrew's observations of Minta, whose "rashness" is both a strength and fault, reveal her character as foolish and self-centered. Like Mrs. Ramsay, Andrew mentions suicide, believing Minta will "kill herself in some idiotic way," foreshadowing not her death, but his.

The Window, Chapter 15

Summary

Mrs. Ramsay expresses worry regarding Nancy's whereabouts, and she questions Prue. In response to her mother's question, Prue Ramsay, "in her considering way," says she thinks Nancy is with Minta Doyle and Paul Rayley: "Yes ... I think Nancy did go with them."

Analysis

This chapter compresses time in its brevity, in that it reduces Mrs. Ramsay's worry into a single sentence. Mrs. Ramsay suffers her anxiety alone, because Mr. Ramsay, who also minimizes Mrs. Ramsay's feelings, has advised her not to worry about the children.

The Window, Chapter 16

Summary

As Mrs. Ramsay readies for dinner, she worries about Nancy, who she thinks is with the tardy walking group. Jasper and Rose knock at her door, wanting to know if Mildred should postpone dinner—Mildred's special *bœuf en daube*. She says no, annoyed with Nancy, Andrew, Paul, and Minta for staying out so late.

While Jasper and Rose pick out jewelry for Mrs. Ramsay, she watches the rooks, wondering why Rose takes choosing jewelry so seriously. She watches two birds fighting over a branch, enjoying how their wings move, "beating out, out, out." "One of the loveliest [sights] of all to her," she feels she fails in describing it "accurately." Mrs. Ramsay thinks Rose has "some hidden reason of her own for attaching great importance" to adorning her with jewelry. She is saddened, thinking she had little to "give in return." The walkers return, and Mrs. Ramsay's annoyance grows. As she descends the stairs, the smell of something burning stops her. The dinner gong sounds.

Analysis

The shift in Mrs. Ramsay's emotions from anxiety to annoyance develops tension as her mind ventures to dark places. Yet she knows the chance of the entire party being "drowned" is unlikely. She—"again"—feels "alone in the presence of her old antagonist, life."

For Mrs. Ramsay, the faux pas of tardiness to dinner illustrates social expectations, the importance of the event to her, and their genteel sophistication. With 15 people expected, Mrs. Ramsay insists they won't postpone dinner for the "Queen of England," acknowledging her tendency to exaggerate, a sign of self-importance. Because Mr. Ramsay has criticized this particular quality, her acknowledgment of this "shared" vice with Jasper alludes to the conflict of what children inherit from their parents. Mr. Ramsay's complaints about her "lies" seem accusatory—attaching a stigma to her sadness—and unsupportive.

The Window, Chapter 17

Summary

As Mrs. Ramsay sits at the head of the table, she directs guests to their seats, wondering, internally, what she has "done" with her life. At the opposite end of the table, she notices her husband sulking. She serves the soup. Feeling responsible for the party's socializing, she talks to William

Bankes. Lily Briscoe observes Mrs. Ramsay "drifting into that strange no-man's land where to follow people is impossible." Thinking Mrs. Ramsay looks "old," Lily Briscoe wonders why her hostess pities Mr. Bankes, a judgment Lily thinks is incorrect, stemming from Mrs. Ramsay's needs rather than real insight. As she thinks of her painting, Lily has an epiphany to move the tree closer to the middle; she moves a salt shaker on a tablecloth flower as a reminder.

Bored by the women's conversation, Charles Tansley finds dinner conversation "superficial." He insists, again, a trip to the lighthouse will be impossible. Annoyed by Tansley's sexism and pessimism, Lily believes he is the "most uncharming human being she had ever met." Mockingly, she asks him to take her to the lighthouse. Knowing Lily dislikes him, he snaps at her, too. Ashamed Lily made him angry, Tansley wants to work in his room. Regretful, he searches for something to say to Mrs. Ramsay, who talks with Mr. Bankes. The two muse over how people drift apart, while Mr. Bankes, too, thinks dinner is a waste of time.

Ignored Tansley is uncomfortable. Aware of social manners Lily smiles, and Mrs. Ramsay asks about his sea-faring experience. He seizes the opportunity to establish himself. Lily begrudgingly asks him to take her to the lighthouse, pleasing Mrs. Ramsay, while Lily internally wanders to human connection: painting. She chooses to be "nice," but believes she and Tansley will "never know" each other. Seeing the salt, her "spirits" rise "so high at the thought of painting tomorrow that she laughed out loud" while Tansley talks.

Mrs. Ramsay wants to talk about the Mannings, but Mr. Bankes avoids the topic. Disappointed, she eavesdrops on conversations in which everyone seems to be listening to others. Against her wishes, Mr. Ramsay remains silent, annoyed because Augustus Carmichael has asked for more soup. However, to her surprise, her husband controls his anger. When she notices Rose and Roger snickering, she asks them to light candles, hoping Mr. Carmichael has not noticed.

The diners adjust to their surroundings, made new by light: fruit, windows, faces. Paul Rayley and Minta Doyle arrive. The main course is served. Minta laments her lost brooch. Mr. Ramsay—finally—speaks, to tease Minta. She acknowledges his admiration, charming him in return.

Mrs. Ramsay feels a pang of jealousy. She wonders if her husband's neediness and her "old" appearance are her fault. Paul fills in Mrs. Ramsay (who wonders whether they are engaged) on the loss of Minta's brooch. Mr. Bankes praises the *bœuf en daube*, which leads to a conversation about French cooking and the use of vegetable skin.

Seeing all the ways Mrs. Ramsay has gotten her way, Lily finds her "absurd" and "irresistible." She contrasts their lives, then hers and Paul's. Paul tells Lily his plan to find Minta's brooch. When Lily asks if she can accompany him, he laughs at her, causing Lily to meditate on love. She thinks she "need not marry, thank Heaven: she need not undergo that degradation."

While others pick at fruit and laugh among themselves, Mrs. Ramsay senses the party is over, waiting for a lull in conversation to clean. She decides she likes Charles Tansley. When she is about to stand, her husband recites a poem. At its close, he turns directly to her and bows. In this moment, she feels he likes her "better" than ever before. He holds the door for her, and she senses the dinner is "already the past."

Analysis

By far the longest chapter, its length anchors the dinner party scene as the novel's heart, a point of climax. The stream-of-consciousness narrative and shifting points of view create an abundance of figurative language, which may jar and estrange readers. William Bankes looks at his hand on the tablecloth as a "mechanic examines a tool beautifully polished and ready for use." Moments later, in conversation with Mrs. Ramsay, he feels like boots "soaked and gone to dry so that you can hardly force your feet into them." It appears as if characters are so challenged by engaging with one another they can no longer articulate how they feel, and thus speak in similes or metaphors. The language has a dizzying and, possibly alienating, effect on the characters and readers as well. The images are original and vivid, so characters and readers may be processing these figures of speech, distracting their attention from the dinner itself.

Additionally, multiple conversations at the dinner table exclude, and thereby alienate, some guests, like Tansley who does not know the social manners involved in making small talk at a dinner party. This distancing intensifies the alienation by putting together in one room for an extended time period 15 characters who struggle to connect one-on-one. The threat of a single misstep destroying the occasion looms: a burnt entrée, laughter, or Shakespeare. While others wish to retreat, Lily has an epiphany at the table, deciding to remedy the "awkward

space" by moving the tree to the middle of her painting, reflecting Mrs. Ramsay's central position. The symbol of the tree represents Mrs. Ramsay and her central position in her home, the life, love, and connection she provides. The painting brings Lily understanding.

Tansley's reassertion about not going to the lighthouse brings up its symbolic inaccessibility. At dinner the guests seem, as Lily calls Mrs. Ramsay, "remote," which is how the lighthouse appears from the house. The extended metaphor, which begins with Mrs. Ramsay "drifting," culminates with her looking to Mr. Bankes, "as if the ship had turned and the sun had struck its sails again." This metaphor evokes an earlier scene in which Mrs. Ramsay holds on to a sight or sound—the third stroke of the lighthouse—to avoid retreating into thoughts.

At the start of dinner Mr. Ramsay's silence confuses Mrs. Ramsay, and she is baffled by her former affection for him. During dinner, she feels "outside" of everything, remote, inaccessible like the lighthouse, to which Tansley has tactlessly referred. This distance Mrs. Ramsay feels enables her to see "things truly," suggesting the love lost toward her husband is lasting, that what she see is reality, not an ideal. The exhaustion from her efforts seems to peak in this scene, graduating to resignation. She allows conversations to happen without her, almost as if she were conducting an experiment to test whether her family and friends can survive without her, foreshadowing her death.

Sometimes she forges a connection between two people and then quickly exits the conversation, representing the importance of her role in creating harmony and thus deepening the theme of love and loss. Later Mrs. Ramsay is the first to exit the room, another foreshadowing of her death, but also a social convention left over from the Victorian era.

Conflict arises as people fail to connect. Mrs. Ramsay, who feels responsible for the dinner's social harmony, enlists the help of her allies. Yet Mr. Ramsay disregards her willing him to talk, showing his stubborn childishness and developing the theme of reality versus the ideal. As guests discuss fishermen's wages, she knows her husband thinks them an important topic, one he can't "sleep for thinking of them," yet he pouts over Mr. Carmichael's request for more soup rather than connect with others.

Sometimes characters come to her aid—Lily, reluctantly, with Charles Tansley; William Bankes because of his secret love for Mrs. Ramsay; and Minta Doyle because of her flirtation with Mr.

Ramsay—without her having to ask when Mr. Ramsay veers into the danger of becoming self-conscious about his pervading lack of success at the mention of William Shakespeare.

Yet many dislike the dinner as they address its shallowness and their own. The situation creates tension and develops the theme of internal life as minds drift and guests wish to be elsewhere—and are in their internal lives. The narration even includes collective thoughts during the party—"All of them ... thought, 'Pray heaven ... my mind may not be exposed.'" The Mannings, a mutual acquaintance of Mrs. Ramsay and Mr. Bankes, come up in conversation. When Mr. Bankes asks Mrs. Ramsay if he should "give her love" to Carrie, her estranged friend with a "new billiard room," she says no, making him think, "friendships, even the best of them, are frail things."

The Window, Chapter 18

Summary

After dinner the guests linger, deciding what to do next. Mrs. Ramsay hurries off, desiring solitude.

In the stairwell she thinks the dinner guests will remember the night. To her annoyance she discovers James and Cam still awake, arguing about the pig skull. The skull's shadows frighten Cam, and James refuses to take it down, shrieking anytime someone touches it. Hoping to please both children, she winds her shawl around the skull. She comforts Cam, whispering descriptions of the skull's new appearance, comparing it to a "beautiful mountain ... with valleys and flowers and bells ringing and birds singing and little goats," until she falls asleep. Reassured the skull is still there, James asks if they are going to the lighthouse. Mrs. Ramsay tells him no. Disappointed she has given him no hope, she knows he will remember the disappointment forever.

She descends the stairwell, and the remaining guests admire her. Prue Ramsay, speaking with adults, transforms into a child again at the sight of her. She tells Mrs. Ramsay they are going to the beach. Possessed by their grand idea, she urges them to go, "saying she only wished she could come too." Instead, she joins her husband.

Analysis

Mrs. Ramsay exits again, annoying Lily Briscoe, who thinks she leaves "at once with an air of secrecy to do something alone." She actually leaves "slowly," developing tension because Lily seems jealous of and angry toward Mrs. Ramsay. Overwhelmed, Mrs. Ramsay watches the elm trees outside. The branches help her "stabilise her position," reinforcing the trees as symbols of life, love, and connection—her roles in life. She ominously thinks her "world" is "changing" and wants to put things "in order" as life around her changes. Yet other than the negative thoughts about Mr. Ramsay during dinner and her sense of being removed from the situation, how exactly her world is changing is unclear. Her frustration with her husband may be a fleeting thought, like so many other conflicting thoughts presented in the narrative.

Again, the time she spends with her children develops her maternal character. She opens and closes the door with care, manages to solve the problem of the skull while making both children happy, hopes Tansley reads quietly so they can sleep well. When she returns to the party, she persists in her motherly airs, asking when she can expect those going to the beach to return and ensuring someone has a watch.

The Window, Chapter 19

Summary

Forgetting what she wanted, Mrs. Ramsay sits and begins knitting. Mr. Ramsay reads. Reflecting on the poem he recited at dinner ("A Garden Song" by Charles Elton), she reads "The Sirens' Song" by William Browne, "zigzagging" down the page. Their eyes meet, but they avoid talking.

Mr. Ramsay decides success in thought does not matter, "A great man, a great book, fame—who could tell?" He refrains from complaining to Mrs. Ramsay, who looks "peaceful." Aware of his gaze, she asks for—if it isn't a bother—more quiet time. He smiles at her, admiring her beauty, but exaggerating her "ignorance" and "simplicity, for he liked to think that she was not ... book-learned at all."

Finished reading, she tells him about Minta Doyle and Paul Rayley's engagement, which he suspected. They sit, silent.

Wishing for him to speak, she jokes about Paul's watch, which amuses him.

He tells her she won't finish the stocking. She agrees, realizing he wants her to tell him she loves him, a struggle for her. She stands at the window, watching the sea. He watches her. Turning to him, smiling, she tells him he was right; they won't be able to go to the lighthouse. She smiles at her success of showing him her love without having to verbalize it.

Analysis

Many of the day's conflicts are resolved by the last chapter of "The Window": Mrs. Ramsay, at the moment, likes Charles Tansley; Minta and Paul, engaged, have returned with Nancy and Andrew Ramsay; Lily Briscoe has resolved not to marry and has decided to move the tree in her painting, giving her more understanding of the painting's subject; the lighthouse trip is settled. What remains are Mr. and Mrs. Ramsay's tensions and the confirmation that they love each other as they are.

Time Passes, Chapter 1

Summary

Leaving the terrace, William Bankes says they must wait for the "future." Arriving from the beach, Andrew Ramsay says, "It's almost too dark to see." Prue Ramsay agrees. Lily Briscoe asks if they should leave the light on. Prue says no—"not if every one's in." She tells Andrew to extinguish the hall light, and the lamps go out, except for Augustus Carmichael's, who likes to read at night.

Analysis

The timeline is ambiguous, but the setting is the summer house, with some of the same characters: Mr. Bankes, Andrew, Prue, Lily, and Mr. Carmichael. It is night, but the ambiguity of darkness and Mr. Bankes's mention of the "future" create tension and foreboding, as though the future is not merely a literal tomorrow.

Readers may expect Mr. and Mrs. Ramsay, but the characters

present wait for no one else. Prue, who becomes childlike in the presence of her mother, acts as the adult here, highlighting the absence of Mrs. Ramsay.

The second part of the novel, "Time Passes," covers the longest span of time, 10 years, in a short number of pages, 10 to 20 or so. The compression of time in this part of the novel serves two purposes: 1) it illustrates the way the characters experience the passage of time; and 2) it suggests the destructive nature of time and the way in which events in time quickly and profoundly affect the lives of the characters. The dark night of these 10 years changes the characters individually and collectively.

Time Passes, Chapter 2

Summary

On a rainy night, darkness descends on the house through "keyholes and crevices." The only stir in the house is the "detached" wind. Exploring the house, it interacts with the falling wallpaper, the trash. It travels up the stairs to the servants' quarters and bedrooms, only to descend the stairs—moving rose petals, spreading sand. An "aimless gust of lamentation" slams the kitchen door. At midnight Augustus Carmichael blows out his candle.

Analysis

The imagery—"the moon sunk, and a thin rain drumming on the roof"—creates a mood of almost ghostly upheaval, of things in the house not being as they should. Details show the same "shabby" house ("rusty hinges and swollen sea-moistened woodwork," "hanging" wallpaper), but the atmosphere is far different. Beginning with a "downpouring of immense darkness," "nothing" moves through the house, ending with a slammed kitchen door. The lyrical language and abstract images, a lamenting wind, reinforce the mood and evoke impending loss.

Augustus Carmichael extinguishing the candle, set in brackets, is the only action in the chapter and parallels the death of Mrs. Ramsay, which is noted in the next chapter.

Time Passes, Chapter 3

Summary

Images of autumn, winter, night, darkness, and destruction continue. Trees are tattered, ravaged. The images of closing curtains, broken treasures, and penitence evoke a mood of chaos and devastation. Mrs. Ramsay died unexpectedly during the night. In the "dark" morning, Mr. Ramsay walks down a hallway, stretching his arms in vain.

Analysis

Time is unclear in this section. After the foreboding images of night (winter nights, autumn nights, what is seen in the moonlight), the darkness continues in the morning with news of Mrs. Ramsay's death. But readers do not know how much time has elapsed. The images of ravaged trees, in particular, symbolize the loss of life, love, and connection embodied in Mrs. Ramsay's existence. The images also reflect the dark, chaotic house, now without its light and its center.

Time Passes, Chapter 4

Summary

The "stray airs" seep into the house again, encountering the things "people have shed and left." There is rarely movement: a loose rock in the valley, a "fold of the shawl" falling loose and swinging. Mrs. McNab arrives to air and clean the house.

Analysis

Remaining artifacts and groaning wood reflect the house's abandonment. The trees' shadows on the bedroom wall recall Mrs. Ramsay and her children watching birds fight over branches. The tree, a symbol of life, represents, with its shadows (a diminished image), Mrs. Ramsay's death and absence, a house no longer imbued with love and loveliness. Mrs. McNab is "directed" to conduct routine cleaning, showing the family managing the house from a distance. No one visits.

Time Passes, Chapter 5

Summary

Approximately 70, Mrs. McNab cleans the house, singing an old popular song wondering, "how long it shall endure?" She stands smiling and cleaning and continues life "as before," drinking and gossiping.

Analysis

This chapter reflects the barrenness of the house and the mortality of its inhabitants. Mrs. McNab can be seen as almost a grotesque reflection, or even ghostly parody, of Mrs. Ramsay. For beautiful, class-conscious Mrs. Ramsay her home was a sanctuary; she fussed over her children and guests who loved her warmth and hospitality. Not vain, Mrs. Ramsay was aware of her beauty but spent little time in front of mirrors.

Now, alone in the house and cleaning under unused beds and in corners, the elderly, worn-out caretaker, Mrs. McNab, attends to the house. Old Mrs. McNab thinks of the tedium of life and sees her ravaged image in the glass, what Mrs. Ramsay always feared. She thinks of her own children and her life, without joy, and not as Mrs. Ramsay would think of her own life and children.

Time Passes, Chapter 6

Summary

Prue Ramsay marries in spring and dies that summer from childbirth complications. Mrs. McNab dusts and sweeps the abandoned house.

In France, Andrew Ramsay, along with approximately 30 other men, dies instantly when a shell explodes. That spring Augustus Carmichael publishes a collection of poems to acclaim.

Analysis

Passing seasons are represented by unpleasant images of
nature: summer winds, flies, gnats, and overgrown gardens.
Late in the summer, the war is represented abstractly with the
shock of dull sounds loosening the shawl and breaking
teacups. Periodically the glass in the cupboard quakes, or a
thud sounds. These little movements represent the distant
explosions of war, foreshadowing Andrew's death.

Time Passes, Chapter 7

Summary

Nights, summer, winters, and years pass: "for night and day,
month and year ran shapelessly together," a description that
reflects the text's concern with both the passage and
perception of time. The only sound in the abandoned house is
lightning. In spring flowers bloom, even though no one is there
to witness them.

Analysis

Nature creates tension. Despite the deaths of Mrs. Ramsay,
Prue, and Andrew, life continues, fleeting. The trees, which
represent life, love, and connection, face the house, "beholding
nothing." All remains empty and hollow.

Time Passes, Chapter 8

Summary

Rumors circulate about the Ramsays selling the house. Not
expecting them to return, Mrs. McNab picks flowers to bring
home. The house and its contents are in disrepair—plaster
falling, books moldy, locks broken, rats. She sees Mrs.
Ramsay's gardening cloak and remembers her employer's
graciousness and the cook, Mildred. Mrs. McNab decides it is
"too much" for her to care for, so she locks up, leaving the
house completely alone.

Analysis

Mrs. McNab's observations and thoughts offer clarity. Because
of the war, travel is hard, making it difficult to employ help to
maintain the house. Mrs. McNab notices it has been left with
the expectation of returning: "a brush and comb left on the
dressing table" with its drawers "full of things." This
observation reveals how death and war have disrupted normal
life. With Mrs. McNab's departure, the house is completely
deserted, with little or no hope for the future—like a town
destroyed by war.

Time Passes, Chapter 9

Summary

The house sits deserted and in continued disrepair. As it is
about to disappear into the "sands of oblivion," Mrs. McNab
receives a letter asking her to prepare the house. She and Mrs.
Bast arrive with cleaning supplies. George, Mrs. McNab's son,
cuts the lawn and traps animals. They employ contractors to
repair the house. "Slowly and painfully" the house is restored.
Mrs. McNab recounts happier times in the house, recalling
once again Mildred the cook. One September evening Lily
Briscoe and Augustus Carmichael arrive.

Analysis

Other than wild things (toads, swallows, butterflies, and thistle),
the lighthouse beam is the only thing that enters the house.
The lighthouse, representing inaccessibility and the multiple
nature of things, illustrates the house's descent into ruin. Mrs.
McNab and the people she hires save the deteriorating house
despite the "pool of Time that was fast closing over them." The
narrator's lyrical descriptions—"some rusty laborious birth
seemed to be taking place"—represent the rebirth of life, the
revitalization of the house.

The treatment of time is reflected in this chapter as it is in the
10 chapters of this section of the book, in contrast to the first
and third sections. The repairs that occur over months are
condensed into a few sentences, whereas part of a day is
extended to 19 chapters.

Time Passes, Chapter 10

Summary

Lily Briscoe falls asleep listening to the sea. Augustus Carmichael reads. When he finishes, he thinks the house looks "much" like he remembers. In the morning Lily opens her eyes "wide" and sits "bolt upright."

Analysis

The familiarity of the guests (Lily's fixation with the sea, Mr. Carmichael's reading) shows their comfort at returning despite time and loss. Their return to the house will force them to come to terms with the absence of Mrs. Ramsay in her domain.

The Lighthouse, Chapter 1

Summary

It is not quite eight o'clock in the morning, 10 years after the beginning of the novel. As Lily Briscoe sits at the table alone, she struggles with her feelings. Mr. Ramsay, Cam, and James are late for their lighthouse expedition. Mr. Ramsay, who stormed out, walks angrily outside. He peers through the window. Lily avoids him. Sitting in the same spot she did at the dinner party, Lily recalls her epiphany to move the tree. Before Mr. Ramsay looks at her again, she retrieves her art supplies.

Lily sets up her easel in the same spot as 10 years before. She decides to paint the picture again; she never finished the first one, and now she knows how to complete it ("move the tree to the middle"), but Mr. Ramsay's sulking distracts her. She pretends she is busy to ward him off, messing with a rag and paint tubes, hoping Cam and James will arrive. Mr. Ramsay stops beside her. She resolves to "give him" what she can.

Analysis

Mr. Ramsay's character introduces most of the conflict. He loses his temper because the children sleep late and Nancy

has forgotten to order lunches. Nancy storms in, "desperate," asking for help: "What does one send to the Lighthouse?" Yet the house remains as is, dumbstruck. Lily sits; Augustus Carmichael pours his coffee and leaves as Mr. Ramsay walks "in a rage," wearing a "distraught wild gaze."

Lily keeps referring to the passage of time (sitting and standing in the same spots), drawing attention to the absences. As she grows angry with Mr. Ramsay for his selfishness, she thinks, "She was dead. The step where she used to sit was empty. She was dead." This repetition of Mrs. Ramsay's death develops the theme of love and loss as Lily continues to grieve.

The trip to the lighthouse recalls the decade-old disagreement about the weather, a battle between genders and between father and son (Mrs. Ramsay and James versus Mr. Ramsay and Charles Tansley). Ten years later, on a "beautiful still day," disagreement looms between father and children, a battle between generations (Mr. Ramsay versus James and Cam). The trip to the inaccessible lighthouse has been delayed for a decade, and the family seems unable to overcome conflict, deepening the enduring tension between Mr. Ramsay and James. James still carries his aversion to his father, exposing their unloving relationship, their inability to connect, and James's Oedipal struggles with his mother's death.

The third part of the novel, "The Lighthouse," stretches time again to cover one morning. The effect of stretching and compressing time continues to emphasize the significance and effects of particular events on the characters. The movement in time throughout the three parts of the novel from afternoon/evening, to night, to morning suggests that the characters are moving toward some resolution to their conflicts.

The Lighthouse, Chapter 2

Summary

Mr. Ramsay observes Lily Briscoe. Seeking her sympathy, he asks if she has everything she wants. She does. They stand in silence, looking at the sea. Baffled by Lily's inattentiveness, Mr. Ramsay groans. Lily ignores him. He sighs and waits, wondering why she hasn't said anything. When he says visiting the lighthouse is "very painful," Lily thinks he is "dramatising himself." In vain he adopts a "pose of extreme decrepitude." Still not knowing what to say, she admires his boots; he starts talking about boots and bootmakers, and then shows her how to tie a knot.

As pity seeps into Lily Briscoe's heart, Cam and James arrive. Imbued with purpose, Mr. Ramsay forgets Lily, who feels "snubbed," and leads his children away.

Analysis

During Lily and Mr. Ramsay's conversation, their missed timing develops tension. In Mr. Ramsay's need for sympathy, Lily could have been any woman, but Mr. Ramsay admittedly likes her; she, knowing how he exhausted Mrs. Ramsay, is unable to speak to him. Presumably caused by disgust or disrespect, this failure distresses her, causing her to think she is "not a woman, but a peevish, ill-tempered, dried-up old maid."

Much of Mr. and Mrs. Ramsay's conflict arose from being opposites: man, woman; provider, protector; mercurial, calm. Now Lily finds herself in Mrs. Ramsay's place, and Mr. Ramsay's presence causes her anxiety. She thinks, as a "woman, she should have known how to deal with it," demonstrating how the gender-based society has influenced her perception of and expectations for herself.

The Lighthouse, Chapter 3

Summary

Looking from the canvas to the garden, Lily Briscoe feels "divided." The image has remained a "knot in her mind" for a decade, and she struggles with the first brushstroke.

Remembering Charles Tansley, who discourages women artists, she recalls a beach day. While writing letters Mrs. Ramsay periodically watches Lily and Tansley skip stones—smiling. Realizing Mrs. Ramsay had choreographed their momentary friendship, Lily calls the memory a "work of art."

As she sees the connection between life and art, Lily fails to discover a revelatory truth, thinking meaning comes from "little daily miracles, illuminations, matches struck unexpectedly in

the dark." She remembers Mrs. Ramsay saying in moments, "Life stand still here," bringing permanence to what might otherwise be forgotten. Thinking "she owed it all to" Mrs. Ramsay, she walks to view the bay and sees Mr. Ramsay, Cam, and James as they hoist the sail.

Analysis

Alone with her painting, Lily struggles with internal conflict, the creative process. She realizes how uncomfortable Mr. Ramsay's lurking had made her (grabbing the wrong paintbrush, setting her easel wrong), keeping her from painting. Nervous, she paints self-consciously, muttering "can't paint, can't write," displaying how deeply Charles Tansley's thoughts have stung. Because her painting symbolizes understanding and catharsis, Lily must finish it to attain both.

As Lily gets lost in the process (losing "consciousness of outer things" such as her name and Mr. Carmichael's presence) she has an emotional epiphany—as "scenes, and names, and sayings, and memories and ideas" arise—she realizes Mrs. Ramsay's role in creation, in her life, in her passion. This understanding furthers the theme of love and loss, as Lily comes to terms with both. Although she hopes no one interrupts her because she wants to continue painting, she is drawn by curiosity and guilt to Mr. Ramsay's excursion.

The Lighthouse, Chapter 4

Summary

The boat hardly moves, and Cam and James hope they will have to turn back. The siblings worry their father's behavior will make Macalister and his son, whom they hired to take them to the lighthouse, "uncomfortable." After Macalister's son rows out farther, the boat takes off.

As Mr. Ramsay and Macalister talk about a big storm in which 11 ships were driven into the bay, Mr. Ramsay becomes engrossed in and connected to the story. Cam admires her father's strength, thinking he would have been among the rescuers, a feeling that threatens her resolve to join her brother in fighting their father's tyranny.

Then reciting the closing lines of William Cowper's "The

Castaway," Mr. Ramsay points out their house to Cam, startling her. He points again. All look, but Cam fails to see it. He mocks and scolds her. Annoyed yet charmed by women, he tries to remedy the situation by asking about their puppy. She answers halfheartedly and then ignores his subsequent question. He reaches for his book, and she stares at the island, remembering his "crass blindness and tyranny."

Analysis

The people on the boat are in close proximity but interact little, their internal lives dominating their external lives, and thus highlighting the lack of connection among them. The one exception is Macalister and Mr. Ramsay's connection during the discussion of the storm.

This social tension in the boat is reminiscent of Mrs. Ramsay's dinner. Because Mr. and Mrs. Ramsay represent oppositions, the events they host reflect these differences: an intimate dinner within the house and an adventurous excursion outdoors.

Forced into Mr. Ramsay's ritual, Cam and James are angry. In "The Window" the siblings fought about the skull, but here, 10 years later at 17 and 16, respectively, they are united, developing their characters and their connection. In response to their father's authoritarian personality, they promise each other to "resist tyranny to the death," thereby deepening the tension and interpersonal connection on the boat.

The Lighthouse, Chapter 5

Summary

Lily Briscoe spots Mr. Ramsay's boat before it launches across the bay. The memory of Mrs. Ramsay writing letters at the beach returns to her, making her wonder why this, of all memories, survives: how Mrs. Ramsay sees something in the distance and grabs for her glasses, asking and guessing what it is. Painting, Lily struggles with space, while in her mind she sits beside Mrs. Ramsay on the beach. Lily imagines updating her about the Rayleys, whose marital troubles she has fabricated: Minta careless and garish; Paul jealous and unfaithful.

Recalling the tension between Lily and her friend regarding marriage, she thinks how despite Mrs. Ramsay's power over people, nothing has turned out the way she intended. As Mrs. Ramsay had wished, she and William Bankes went on walks but remained friends. She keeps looking at the house steps, which because of Mrs. Ramsay's death seem empty. Again Lily yearns to talk to Augustus Carmichael. These desires culminate in her thoughts: "to want and not to have—to want and want—how that wrung the heart." Mourning her friend and searching for meaning, she begins to cry, thinking "all was miracle," that no one knows a thing. Tears flowing, she cries out for Mrs. Ramsay.

Analysis

Lily Briscoe explores her internal conflict while painting, in an attempt to come to terms with her life and Mrs. Ramsay's death. Her uninterrupted thoughts flow from Mrs. Ramsay to Minta Doyle to Paul Rayley, deepening the theme of internal life by revealing the pain that has remained dormant. Though Lily, for once, does not want to be alone, her inability to console Mr. Ramsay plagues her, distracting her from painting. She wants to talk to Mr. Carmichael, who reclines on his chair, but his hat is tipped over his face, making him inaccessible and spiraling Lily deeper into thought.

Searching for the reason Mrs. Ramsay is obsessed with marriage, Lily—thinking about love—sees Paul, a fire protruding from him. Any time love has arisen in Lily's mind over the decade, "Paul's fire" burns, "the roar and the crackle," developing her unrequited love for him, her character, and the theme of love and loss.

The Lighthouse, Chapter 6

Summary

The entire chapter appears in brackets, as if the action is an afterthought to the main text. After Macalister's son catches a fish, he cuts a chunk from its body to bait his hook and throws its body back into the sea: "The mutilated body (it was still alive) was thrown back into the sea."

Analysis

Typically, the narrator uses brackets to include factual information, which here suggests little is happening on the boat, inwardly and outwardly. The language suggests a certain brutality in the act, or in survival itself.

The bracketed text also suggests that the action is meaningless to Macalister's son; the toss back into the sea is written in the passive voice, as if he is not an active participant. Yet the inclusion of this chapter suggests this compressed moment in time may have an effect on another character.

The Lighthouse, Chapter 7

Summary

Lily Briscoe is grateful no one hears her crying and calling for Mrs. Ramsay. The "pain of want" and her "bitter anger" lessen. Briefly she feels Mrs. Ramsay's presence bringing her relief. She returns to painting, imagining Mrs. Ramsay surrounded by flowers.

Desiring "distance and blue," Lily looks to the water and sees Mr. Ramsay's boat in the middle of the bay.

Analysis

Noticing the considerable distance between the boat and lighthouse, Lily wonders whether they will reach their destination, a journey that parallels for them what completing her painting means for her. Thinking the "sea and sky" look made of "one fabric," disoriented, she momentarily loses sight of the boat and feels anxious, wanting to connect more with Mr. Ramsay.

The Lighthouse, Chapter 8

Summary

The sail loses the wind, stalling the boat. Without wind, movement, and sound to distract everyone, the group becomes aware of each other, except for Mr. Ramsay, who reads. Cam thinks, "Everything in the whole world seemed to stand still."

In thinking about his father, James realizes it is not Mr. Ramsay he wants to kill but the dark rages that overcome his father. James begins to understand that his father's behavior toward him and others is not his father's fault; his father is a victim of a higher, uncontrollable force. Using the image of the wagon wheel crushing someone's foot, James realizes he cannot blame the wheel. For James the wheel was his father's crushing ("It will rain," Mr. Ramsay had said) of his childish yearning to go to the lighthouse: a "silvery, misty-looking tower with a yellow eye that opened suddenly and softly in the evening." He sees the lighthouse clearly now from the boat—a stark and straight black and white tower, with laundry drying on the rocks.

James waits for his father to "say something sharp," but he doesn't. As James senses his father's awareness, the sail catches wind, and the boat moves again.

Analysis

The stalled boat parallels James's internal life. Stalled emotionally by hatred for his father, he reflects on old but continuing anger, stalled in time. The anger centers on the lighthouse, which for James represents the inaccessible, something far different from the unremarkable tower he sees now. Accepting the reality of both—a mystery of his childhood and a commonplace reality of the present time—James seems able to accept the multiplicity of vision and understanding.

That multiplicity applies to his relationship with his father as well. By understanding that his father's tyranny is something more than deliberate behavior toward him, James can come to terms with the subjective reality of his father at the same time as he continues to long for his mother, a memory in which his father's presence intrudes but does not destroy.

As the wind picks up and the boat moves, James's thoughts parallel the boat's movement, allowing him to move on as well, toward the lighthouse and toward resolution.

The Lighthouse, Chapter 9

Summary

As Lily Briscoe gazes at the still and peaceful sea that "stretche[s] like silk across the bay," she worries over the power of distance. She cannot find Mr. Ramsay's boat, and she fears her friends are "gone for ever ... becom[ing] part of the nature of things."

Analysis

The chapter is enclosed in brackets, signifying an external observation. The structure suggests Lily is completely invested in finding the boat. Her fear alludes to the unaddressed trauma of Mrs. Ramsay's death, developing the theme of love and loss. As she searches for the group whom she fears may be "swallowed up" by the sea, she seems afraid to lose more.

The Lighthouse, Chapter 10

Summary

Cam watches the shore from the sea. She begins telling herself a story of escaping from a sinking ship because she craves "adventure and escape." James watches the sail, and she wants to tell him to consider their father as he is now (reading), to temper James's negative opinions. Mr. Ramsay looks up to "pin down some thought more exactly." She continues with her adventure story, looking back at the shore, whispering "how we perished, each alone."

Analysis

Cam reaches peace in her thoughts—no longer hurt by her father's offensiveness and brother's stubbornness, which cause her "anguish"—and considers what is next after feeling "all had slipped, all had passed, all had streamed away." Cam, like her mother, fears old age and loneliness. These thoughts, like James's in Chapter 8, display emotional growth.

Observing Mr. Ramsay in memory (an "intolerably egotistical" and "sarcastic brute") and at present ("reading the little book with his legs curled"), she does not see a "vain tyrant." She sees an old man, someone who ensures she is comfortable, and she can accept him as he is now. Like Lily Briscoe and painting, Cam creates, inventing an adventure story. Her narrative represents how she aligns more with modern women than with the gender roles her parents represent. At the same time, she repeats something her father says, "how we perished, each alone," showing how part of him lives in her.

The Lighthouse, Chapter 11

Summary

As Lily Briscoe thinks "so much ... depends on distance," she watches Mr. Ramsay's boat move across the bay. Augustus Carmichael grunts, retrieves his book, and continues reading. Barely able to spot them, Lily thinks they will land at the lighthouse before lunch and returns to her painting, not wanting to be interrupted.

Noting how Mr. Carmichael has changed and not changed, Lily feels they are connected by thoughts, despite her knowing him only vaguely—the outline, not the details. She thinks both of how Andrew's death affected him and of his current recognition, although she has never read his poetry. She recalls he did not care much for Mrs. Ramsay and was unaffected by her. Her thoughts then turn to Charles Tansley, her dislike of him, Mrs. Ramsay's treatment of him, and his antiwar advocacy. She sees him in her own way and for her own purposes, which for her are in the role of a whipping boy. But that is not necessarily how others view him.

While observing and fussing with a trail of ants, Lily wishes for "fifty pairs of eyes" to understand. She thinks, "Fifty pairs of eyes were not enough to get round that one woman with." She ponders the memory of Mr. Ramsay gallantly proposing to Mrs. Ramsay and then their marriage, which "was no monotony of bliss," recalling their arguments, "long rigid" silences, and how Mr. Ramsay bothered Mrs. Ramsay until she spoke to him again. Their petty differences and deeper conflict appear in her "impulses and quicknesses; he with his shudders and glooms."

Someone enters the drawing room. The person's shadow creates a "triangular shadow" on the step—recalling how Lily represented Mrs. Ramsay reading to James in her first painting—which slightly changes the "composition of the picture." Dipping her brush, she remembers her former "mood," thinking someone wants to see the ordinary (a "chair") as it is, but recognize simultaneously it is also miraculous. Her torment returns after her inspiration, the new shape on the porch, is altered by the wind, letting the image escape her. She recalls the Ramsays again and Prue's short-lived happiness. She sees Mrs. Ramsay again, amid flowers, and cries for her. Then Lily walks to the lawn's edge to look for the boat and Mr. Ramsay.

Analysis

Facing the external conflict of balancing Mrs. Ramsay and the painting, which will bring her understanding and catharsis of grief, Lily is filled with the sensation things are "happening for the first time." This feeling creates tension between memory and the present, as she searches for what evades her.

As Lily sifts through her memory, she remembers Mr. Ramsay's tyrannical nature, giving her insight into Cam's and James's anger toward their father. She remembers how the "bedroom door would slam violently early in the morning," displaying how Mr. Ramsay's wrath would begin as soon as he woke, making Cam and James's pact reasonable.

Through her memories, Lily recalls the extent to which Mrs. Ramsay protected her children, and the source of the family's peace becomes apparent. Lily remembers how often Mr. and Mrs. Ramsay wandered off to the pear trees to "have it out together." The setting is significant here because the trees symbolize the life, love, and connection between husband and wife and between mother and children. Being in harmony with her husband and fulfilling her role as a wife enable her to fulfill her role as a mother.

Lily's statement about distance applies not only to her sighting of the boat, but of life and understanding in general. One cannot see or understand people or events when one is too close to them. The statement is only part of the author's vision, for not only does one need distance, but one needs "fifty pairs of eyes" to see the many simultaneous and often conflicting facets not only of Mrs. Ramsay but of people and events.

As Lily confronts her issues, she comes closer to understanding the complexity of life and the balance in the painting, inching closer to understanding herself—"so full her

mind was of what she was thinking, of what she was seeing."

The Lighthouse, Chapter 12

Summary

James observes Mr. Ramsay, close to finishing his book, and thinks he looks old, the physical manifestation of "what was always at the back of both their minds"—"loneliness." Approaching the lighthouse, James is satisfied and repeats something his father has said, "We are driving before a gale—we must sink." Bored, Cam watches her father read, oblivious to them, and dozes off. Hungry, Mr. Ramsay startles Cam, demanding, "Come now."

Macalister praises James for his control of the boat, but James is annoyed his father never compliments him. Feeling safe, Cam eats an egg, adding to her story, as Mr. Ramsay and Macalister discuss the war. Mr. Ramsay scolds Cam for almost throwing her sandwich overboard and tells her to save it. She reacts as though he has said something wise, of which she approves, and he gives her a gingerbread nut from his own lunch.

Finally, Macalister's son speaks, pointing out where three men drowned in the storm. James and Cam think their father will recite poetry, which they hate. To their surprise, he doesn't. Mr. Ramsay compliments James on his steering. As they prepare to land, two men wait at the lighthouse, and James and Cam watch Mr. Ramsay looking back at the island, thinking, "Ask us anything and we will give it you." But he is silent. He then asks his children to carry the parcels Nancy packed. They obey and prepare to follow him as he jumps "lightly like a young man ... on to the rock."

Analysis

In the novel's denouement, the group arrives at the previously inaccessible lighthouse, bringing the mounting tension over the bad weather and human interaction to rest and offering resolution.

James faces his emotional conflict, reflecting the Freudian Oedipal theories of early childhood, his murderous rages being the natural reaction to a father's interference in a boy's desire for intimacy with his mother. Reflection helps James recognize he and his father are similar: both are lonely; both have now shared a close view of the lighthouse. As James faces the structure he was once so passionate about, he realizes it is a "stark tower on a bare rock," and he repeats one of his father lines, "exactly as his father said it," showing deep contemplation and acceptance.

After Mr. Ramsay compliments James on his sailing, Cam, torn between them, thinks "There! ... You've got it at last." Even though James looks "sulky" and frowns, Cam knows he does not want to "share a grain of pleasure," illuminating their bond, a milestone between father and son, and another confirmation of their similarity. Earlier Cam pondered Mr. Ramsay's inaccessibility—like the lighthouse's. Now they arrive at what has seemed impossible, or inaccessible, for them throughout the novel: the lighthouse trip and human connection.

Through Mr. Ramsay's approval of his sailing, James and his father are able to connect. James may already have forgiven, or at least come to terms with, his father and his failures. In this scene, Cam, who knows her brother better than the other passengers do, believes he is content, but he does not reveal this emotion.

It is up to the reader to decide how much James has accepted and where he is emotionally. Certainly his vision is broader and his acceptance greater—he sees the lighthouse as it was to him and as it is now—but he is still young and may need more distance, which he and Cam maintain somewhat, for although they rise to follow their father, they are still in the boat at the end of the novel. Readers may wonder whether Mr. Ramsay, with his newfound energy, will help them disembark or leave them to do it on their own, affirming their independence. Either way, they will disembark, and James, like Cam earlier in the excursion, has moved toward accepting his father and his father accepting him in their journey toward understanding and connection.

The Lighthouse, Chapter 13

Summary

Lily Briscoe assumes the boat has reached the lighthouse and thinks Mr. Ramsay has received the sympathy she failed to give him that morning. Augustus Carmichael joins her at the lawn's edge and says, "They will have landed." Lily is comforted by knowing they are thinking the same things, and "he had answered her without her asking him anything."

Exhausted, Lily returns to her canvas. Looking between the "blurred" painting and the "empty" steps, with "sudden intensity" she paints a line in the center of the canvas, finishing the piece.

Analysis

Lily and Mr. Carmichael share a profound moment of ease over knowing, individually then together, Mr. Ramsay's boat has reached the lighthouse, that Mr. Ramsay, James, and Cam have reached what was previously inaccessible. Their connection satisfies Lily, showing the growth of both characters, who throughout the novel have struggled to connect with others.

Almost simultaneously Lily is able to complete her painting, as she reaches her own understanding of its subject and comes to terms with her years of grieving. Lily's vision, which now satisfies her, is equivalent to James, Cam, and Mr. Ramsay arriving at the lighthouse. As she finishes her painting, she realizes she does not care where it is hung, but she knows that it captures for eternity the essence of a single moment. The moment and her vision of it will endure long after all are gone.

❝❞ Quotes

"It was a thousand pities."

— Narrator, The Window, Chapter 9

Mr. Ramsay scares Lily Briscoe with his mood swings, and William Bankes consoles her by contemplating Mr. Ramsay's tempestuousness. As he speaks William Bankes reflects on the others Mr. Ramsay harms with his tyrannical nature. Secretly in love with Mrs. Ramsay, Mr. Bankes pities Lily who gets caught in the wake of his anger: Mrs. Ramsay who caters to Mr. Ramsay's neediness; the Ramsay children who are subjected to their father's erratic behavior; and himself, who mourns his estranged friendship with Mr. Ramsay and perhaps thinks himself a better partner for Mrs. Ramsay.

"The sky stuck to them; the birds sang through them."

— Narrator, The Window, Chapter 9

As Lily Briscoe watches Mr. and Mrs. Ramsay "being in love," she excitedly witnesses their emotions and how the world appears to revolve around them. Mrs. Ramsay's world certainly does revolve around her, together with her husband. Lily loves and envies them.

"A light here required a shadow there."

— Narrator, The Window, Chapter 9

William Bankes shows interest in the purple triangular shape in Lily Briscoe's painting. Lily says it is Mrs. Ramsay reading to James and explains the process of shading. Harboring romantic feelings for Mrs. Ramsay and scientific-minded, Mr. Bankes is intrigued and questions her representation, but Lily cannot articulate or visualize her intention "without a brush in her hand." Taken at face value, her words pertain to the painting technique; however, beyond their literal meaning, she may be referring both to multiple perspectives and to balance (what eludes her in the composition), indicating that something dark is countered by contrasting lightness, or more broadly a negative by a positive, or opposing condition.

"She could be herself, by herself."

— Narrator, The Window, Chapter 11

Mildred takes James from Mrs. Ramsay. Because of the roles she has assumed for herself, because of the way others see and need her, and because her external life conflicts with her internal life, Mrs. Ramsay takes great pleasure in the few minutes she has to be alone and not playing a part.

"[S]he made him believe that he

could do whatever he wanted. He had felt her eyes on him all day today, following him about (though she never said a word) as if she were saying, "Yes, you can do it. I believe in you. I expect it of you.""

— Narrator, The Window, Chapter 14

After Paul Rayley proposes to Minta Doyle, he wants to tell Mrs. Ramsay, who encouraged him. His thoughts reveal the power Mrs. Ramsay has over others. Her positive energy and wordless encouragement lead others to do as she believes they should, for better or worse. Even if not all follow Mrs. Ramsay's ideas, her influence affects them deeply, and they believe in her love.

"He went to the heart of things."

— Narrator, The Window, Chapter 17

At dinner Charles Tansley and William Bankes discuss a political issue. Bored and drained from keeping the conversation going among her guests, Mrs. Ramsay hopes her husband will contribute something of his sharp political insights. But as she admires his knowledge, he disappoints her with silence and an angry scowl because Augustus Carmichael has asked for more soup.

"Everything seemed possible. Everything seemed right."

— Narrator, The Window, Chapter 17

During dinner Mrs. Ramsay, seeing how much William Bankes and Lily Briscoe have in common, regrets not seating them next to each other. She plans to arrange a walk or picnic for them the following day. She is matchmaking again and once again, shortsighted and mistaken in her ideas about the two characters. Independent Lily has little interest in marriage, and William Bankes is in love with Mrs. Ramsay. This observation parallels her influence in Paul Rayley's and Minta Doyle's engagement.

"Life stand still here."

— Mrs. Ramsay, The Lighthouse, Chapter 3

When Mrs. Ramsay choreographs a moment on the beach in which Charles Tansley and Lily Briscoe share a friendly moment skipping stones, she wants to remember it. The statement is important because Mrs. Ramsay does not want time to pass; she does not want her children to get older or for anything to change.

"They're happy like that; I'm happy like this. Life has changed completely."

— Narrator, The Lighthouse, Chapter 5

Lily Briscoe mourns Mrs. Ramsay, reflecting on the distance she feels between her life and her friend's "old-fashioned" beliefs. She imagines someone trying to update her on all that has occurred in the last decade. Seeing the distance between Mrs. Ramsay and herself, Lily is able to accept who she is.

"Love had a thousand shapes."

— Narrator, The Lighthouse, Chapter 11

Lily Briscoe ponders the "feeling of completeness" that inspired her a decade ago when she began the painting and fell in love with everything around her at the Ramsays' home. Her statement reflects the many ways that love, as well as other emotions, can be felt, understood, and expressed.

Symbols

Lighthouse

Across the bay the lighthouse represents inaccessibility. It appears in the opening scene, creating conflict between Mr. and Mrs. Ramsay and murderous rage from young James. Over 10 years, the long sweep of the light—Mrs. Ramsay believes the light emanates from her—reaches the Ramsays' house, becoming a comfort and a curse to the characters.

With multiple meanings, the lighthouse represents what the main characters find inaccessible at first, but later accessible, or "enlightening." Lily finishes her painting, and James and Cam Ramsay reach a connection with their father. In "The Lighthouse," Chapter 8, James observes the lighthouse, once an unattainable "passion," thinking, "So that was the Lighthouse, was it?" Observing its "stark and straight" structure, he decides the lighthouse in front of him is also the lighthouse of his memories, an "opening and shutting" eye reaching their summer house, "For nothing was simply one thing." His reconciliation of the past and present images of the lighthouse typify the novel's multiple viewpoints that truth, or understanding, is not one-dimensional and that what is inaccessible to one character is not the same for others.

Painting

Painting represents understanding and catharsis. Lily Briscoe paints a scene that includes Mrs. Ramsay reading to James in the drawing room. She ponders Mrs. Ramsay's character, who is "like a bird for speed, an arrow for directness," a "commanding" presence opening windows and shutting doors. Not attempting a "likeness" but rather another sense of "mother and child," she depicts Mrs. Ramsay as a purple triangular shadow. Later Mrs. Ramsay in "The Window," Chapter 11, describes herself as a "wedge of darkness," which resembles a purple triangular shadow.

Lily navigates the issue of balance in the painting. Working on the composition, she achieves a certain understanding by moving the tree (symbolizing love, life, and connection, which for Lily show themselves in Mrs. Ramsay) to a more prominent position to reflect the Mrs. Ramsay's essence and importance.

The act of painting represents catharsis for Lily. At the beginning of the novel, she is anxious about showing the painting to others. Introverted and sensitive, she is unsure about her abilities and intimidated by Charles Tansley's derogatory comments about women's inabilities as artists. Although she continues painting, Lily cannot achieve complete catharsis—for her, the inaccessible—until she fully understands her feelings about Mrs. Ramsay.

When Lily finally allows herself sufficient distance, she is able to finish the new painting with a simple line down the center, achieving the complete sense of balance she has sought, and she can accept herself as an artist. If she achieves understanding in "The Window," she achieves catharsis in "The Lighthouse," as she finishes the painting at the same time as Mrs. Ramsay's husband and children reach the lighthouse.

Tree

While the pear tree receives the most attention in the novel, it is noteworthy that the summer house is surrounded by trees. Representing love, life, and connection, trees protect the home and those in it, as does Mrs. Ramsay.

In "The Window," Chapter 4, Lily Briscoe and William Bankes pause by the pear tree, discussing Mr. Ramsay's stalled career, a discussion showing the intimacy of their deep friendship. At that spot Lily imagines a kitchen table—which, because of Andrew Ramsay's explanation of Mr. Ramsay's field, represents the patriarch and his work—"lodged" in the tree. Lily's image, considering her love for the Ramsays, illustrates how Mr. Ramsay's difficult professional life and demanding presence harm the family's well-being.

When Lily changes the composition of her painting by moving the tree closer to the center, she affirms the tree's importance as a representation of the inner spirit of Mrs. Ramsay, which Lily is trying to capture: the love, life, and connection that make her a nurturing, protecting, and stabilizing force in others' lives.

 # Themes

Love and Loss

Whether the love is familial (James and Mrs. Ramsay), lustful (Paul Rayley and Minta Doyle), marital (Mr. Ramsay and Mrs. Ramsay), platonic (William Bankes and Mr. Ramsay), or unrequited (Lily Briscoe and Paul Rayley; William Bankes and Mrs. Ramsay), each character contemplates love and copes with loss in individual ways. Often characters miss opportunities to connect with one another, making reflection their only expression of love or loss, which is witnessed through the shifting point of view and stream-of-consciousness style. This isolation represents an almost constant loss throughout the novel.

In "The Window," Chapter 19, Mrs. Ramsay senses Mr. Ramsay wants her to tell him she loves him, desiring the "thing she always found it so difficult to give him." Unable to articulate her love, she tells him he was right about the rainy weather, which is her way of connecting with him. Typically, where others may fail to connect, Mrs. Ramsay succeeds merely by being present. Therefore, the absence caused by her death is all the more pervasive.

Sometimes unconscious or seemingly unrelated actions reveal love and loss. In "The Window," Chapter 9, while Mr. Bankes complains about Mr. Ramsay to Lily Briscoe, he quietly admires Mrs. Ramsay, making Lily aware of his unrequited love. In "Time Passes," Chapter 6, quiet Augustus Carmichael, grieved by Andrew Ramsay's death, publishes a well-received poetry collection. A decade later in "The Lighthouse," Lily completes a new painting of Mrs. Ramsay, and Mr. Ramsay takes James to the lighthouse. These final actions reveal not only love for Mrs. Ramsay but acceptance of her death and an affirmation of the love, life, and connection she inspired.

Internal Life

Because of the novel's stream-of-consciousness style and shifting point of view, most of the "plot" unfolds in the minds of the characters. Very little outward action occurs. Indeed, the plot is driven not by what characters do but by what they observe, think, and feel, thus defining their existence.

Mrs. Ramsay may be the most obvious character whose internal and external lives conflict. Externally, she is a devoted mother, compassionate neighbor and benefactor, and sympathetic and sensitive wife. She performs these roles with calm and grace; however, her internal life is chaotic, as conflicting thoughts and emotions battle. As she directs guests to their seats at her dinner party, she feels far removed from the task, asking herself what she has done with her life. The role she has created for herself and in which others see her is not what it appears.

During one-on-one encounters, characters are alienated by their own or others' isolation, or lack of connection. In "The Window," Chapter 10, Cam Ramsay ignores Mrs. Ramsay when she calls her, making Mrs. Ramsay wonder what her daughter is dreaming about, standing in front of her "with some thought of her own." Mrs. Ramsay compares talking to Cam with dropping a message into a well, showing their lack of connection, and she asks her daughter to repeat the message to ensure she listened to her.

Mr. Ramsay's internal life, too, is one of insecurity and continual need for praise and reassurance. He seeks admiration from his followers, who are few, and comfort from his wife, who supplies it. He knows, internally, the reality of his limited intellect will lead to no great contributions in his field. Externally, however, he acts like the "philosopher" he aspires to be, and in his demands for attention from those around him, he is cranky and belligerent, causing murderous emotions in his son and antipathy in others.

Reality versus the Ideal

Many of the characters in the novel consider ideals. During the summer holiday each one—whether pursuits are professional, artistic, domestic, or romantic—makes an effort to organize what and whom they encounter to extract beauty or truth. After the dinner party in "The Window" Mrs. Ramsay enjoys a moment of silence in the stairwell where she tries to extract the "thing that mattered" from the dinner. Wanting to "detach it; separate it off; clean it of all the emotions and odds and ends,"

she wants to possess it, the dinner's ideal, to understand how she and others will remember it. In reality, however, it is a dinner party not unlike others and already a memory.

Throughout the novel, Lily Briscoe labors to represent Mrs. Ramsay and James, their shape and color. Struggling through her creative process and impressions, she tries to create a truth, which she knows, in "The Window," Chapter 9, is not a "likeness" but a "vision ... she had seen clearly once."

📖 Suggested Reading

Bloom, Harold. *Virginia Woolf's To the Lighthouse*. New York: Chelsea, 1988. Print.

Briggs, Julia. *Virginia Woolf: An Inner Life*. New York: Harvest, 2005. Print.

Davies, Stevie. *Woolf's To the Lighthouse*. New York: Penguin: 1989. Print.

Harris, Alexandra. *Virginia Woolf*. New York: Thames & Hudson, 2011. Print.

Matar, Hisham. "The Unsaid: The Silence of Virginia Woolf." *The New Yorker*. Condé Nast, 10 Nov. 2014. Web. 8 Oct. 2016.

Pease, Allison. *The Cambridge Companion to To the Lighthouse*. Cambridge: Cambridge UP, 2014. Print.

Printed in Great Britain
by Amazon